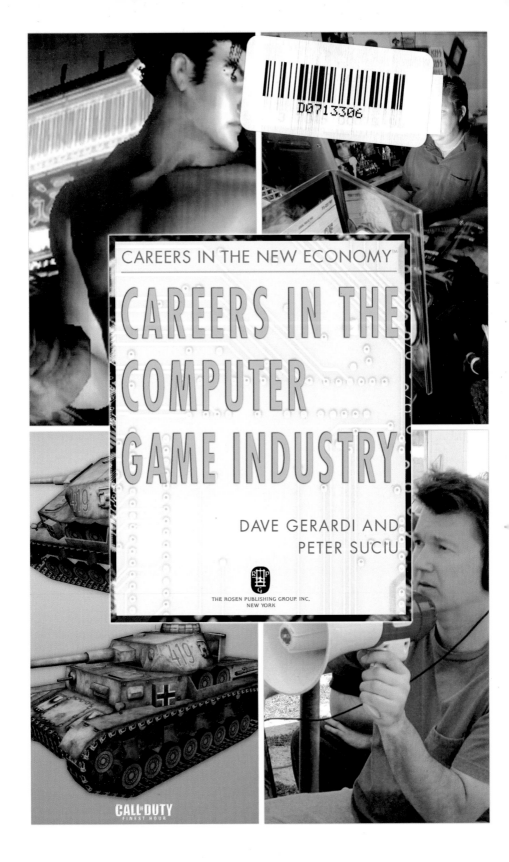

CAREERS IN THE NEW ECONOMY™

CAREERS IN THE COMPUTER GAME INDUSTRY

DAVE GERARDI AND
PETER SUCIU

THE ROSEN PUBLISHING GROUP INC.
NEW YORK

CALL**DUTY**
FINEST HOUR

Published in 2005 by The Rosen Publishing Group, Inc.
29 East 21st Street, New York, NY 10010

Copyright © 2005 by The Rosen Publishing Group, Inc.

First Edition

Library of Congress Cataloging-in-Publication Data

Suciu, Peter.
Careers in the computer game industry/Peter Suciu and Dave Gerardi.
    p. cm.—(Careers in the new economy)
Includes bibliographical references and index.
ISBN 1-4042-0252-8 (library binding)
1. Computer games—Programming. 2. Computer games—Programming—
Vocational guidance. 3. Electronic games industry—United States.
I. Gerardi, David. II. Title. III. Series.
QA76.76.C672S75 2004
794.8'1526—dc22

        2004011258

Manufactured in the United States of America

On the front cover: Left to right: John Riccitiello, president of the computer game development company Electronic Arts; student Benny Soo playing the online computer game *Counter Strike*; a screen shot of the computer game *Amped 2* by Microsoft.

On the back cover: Left to right: "Student Pavilion," a computer-generated image created by Benjamin Lindau; Adrian Smith, co-creator of the computer game *Tomb Raider*; quality assurance testers working on *Uru: Ages Beyond the Myst*.

Photo credits: Front and back cover, pp. 1 (top left and right), 3 (top and third from top), 34, 43, 56, 66, 90, 101, 112 © AP/World Wide Photo; pp. 1 (bottom left), 3 (second from top) © 2003–2004 Activision, Inc., and its affiliates; p. 1 (bottom right) © Photo of sound designer Jack Grillo, courtesy of Mike Mantarro, senior publicist for Activision, Inc.; pp. 3 (fourth from top), 9 © *The SIMs* ® 2004 Electronic Arts and Maxis, courtesy of Brooke Cahalane; pp. 4–5, 118, 120, 139, 140, 142 © Nelson Sá; p. 23 © Tom Wagner/Corbis; pp. 26, 67 courtesy of DigiPen Institute of Technology; pp. 28, 44, 77, 79, 80, 85 © *Call of Duty* ® 2003–2004 Activision, Inc., and its affiliates; p. 76 © Pablo Corral/Corbis; p. 107 courtesy of Steve Bauman and *Computer Games* magazine.

Designer: Nelson Sá; **Editor:** Joann Jovinelly; **Photo Researcher:** Nelson Sá

CONTENTS

INTRODUCTION

If you think you have a great idea for a game, get in line. You are just one of many computer game enthusiasts who feel the same way. The truth is that no company is interested in hiring anyone who makes this claim, no matter how enthusiastic he or she is. Industry insiders hear this line all the time. What's more, they have their own people who have great ideas for games. They don't need people with ideas, they need people who can realize their ideas. You can solidly impress any computer game publishing company if you can execute your ideas from concept to program. This book will explain how computer games are made, who is involved in their creation, and what you can do to get a job in the computer game industry, one of the fastest growing markets in the United States.

With annual sales topping $20 billion worldwide, computer games aren't just kids' stuff anymore. Long gone are the days of popping in a quarter to shoot a few badly rendered aliens creeping toward the bottom of the screen. Today's titles are epic and engrossing, with realistic worlds and stories. Many are complicated, both in the way complex characters travel through the environment and in the way their stories unfold with twisting plots.

Computer games are no longer just played by teenage boys and girls in their parents' basements. Nor do all games require endless hours of play for the possibility of enjoyment. Many are more like interactive movies— there are games aimed at kids for both education and

pure entertainment, while most others are aimed at an older, young adult market.

However, superficial stereotypes about the ways in which computer games are created still remain. For example, many people don't consider the idea of making games for a living a serious career choice. Others simply find the process mysterious and impenetrable, since they are unable to readily find the information or resources needed to get started. This book will fill in the blanks and wipe away any sense of mystery.

To succeed in the computer game industry, you'll need creativity, vision, and the desire to work long hours. Like the film industry, computer games are not made by one or two people, but by entire teams of talented professionals, all with unique skills. No matter what part of the business interests you, you've got to know games. That doesn't mean you have to know every game ever created, but you must familiarize yourself with the different types of games and how they are played.

Sports are a huge genre in the computer game world. In fact, almost 20 percent of console games are sports related, according to the Entertainment Software Association (ESA). Many of these games are based on real-life sports, such as National Football League (NFL) football (*Madden*) or National Basketball Association (NBA) basketball (*Inside Drive*). These titles attempt to re-create the sport as realistically as possible, and are often modeled from players on professional teams. Other games sacrifice realism in favor of over-the-top craziness. For example, *NBA Jam* boasts ridiculous dunks and superhuman moves. In *MLB Slugfest*, a pitcher's fastball literally catches on fire. Other sports games are a combination of both fantasy and reality. *Tony Hawk's Pro Skater* games allow players to compete against the pros, but they also offer the opportunity to skate in unusual places that would never be possible in reality.

The first-person shooter is another popular genre. In this style of play, you dash through the game without seeing your character. You may see a gun or hand on the bottom of the screen, and this points outward at the bad guys (*Doom, Medal of Honor*, and *Halo* are examples). These types of games take place from the first-person point of view. They are typically very action-packed games that rely on speed.

A real-time strategy game like *The Sims* is one in which you typically have an overview of a large map. You may run a country, city, or an army of warriors. You gather resources to pay for the construction of buildings or the maintenance of armies so that you can wage war on your enemies. It all happens in real-time, meaning that you don't take turns and wait until the other player is finished to make your move—you have to be a quick thinker.

Another category of computer game is one that engages the player in role-playing. These games are very similar to pen and paper role-playing games such as *Dungeons and Dragons*. Often you will create a character or a group of characters and explore cities, dungeons, and kingdoms while fighting hordes of bad guys. As you progress through the game, your characters become more experienced and powerful until they are strong enough to defeat the villains. *Final Fantasy, EverQuest,* and *Baldur's Gate* are examples of games in this genre.

Racing games such as *Crimson Skies* and *Mario Kart* are also very popular. Depending on the game, you may be racing cars, trucks, planes, futuristic vehicles, or animals through twisting and turning mazes. There are often "power-ups" to grab. These icons pop up from time to time on the screen. If you run over one, you "pick it up" and it empowers you in a specific way for a brief period, such as giving you extra speed, a smoke screen, a rocket launcher, or whatever else the game's designers have conjured up.

Platform adventure games are one of the most popular and diverse genres. These began as rather simple two-dimensional (2-D) side scrolling programs, meaning you could only move left or right on the screen. Early successes such as *Pitfall* and *Super Mario Brothers* had players jumping over obstacles and discovering hidden treasures, secret objects, and paths to new levels. These have since become grand three-dimensional (3-D) adventures. You can navigate enormous worlds with hundreds of various screens. That old favorite, Mario, is still around, but Sonic the Hedgehog, Crash Bandicoot, Link from the *Legend of Zelda*, and literally dozens of other characters have joined him. While the setting and tone of the adventure may change, one thing is for sure: platform games will have players jumping and running for many years to come.

Fighting games have always been good, button-mashing fun, but the *Mortal Kombat* series took them to the next level. Gruesome finishing moves, such as decapitations, reward players who have memorized secret button combinations to execute the bloody maneuvers. Advances in graphics took the realism factor to a whole new realm. In addition to heightened levels of blood and violence, the characters were much more lifelike, with some games sporting female characters noted more for their skimpy clothing than for their fighting skills. Some titles focused on hand-to-hand combat (*Dead or Alive*), others on weapons (*Soul Calibur*), but the core goal remained: destroy the opposition.

These are the most common types of computer game categories. If you are interested in pursuing a career in the game industry, you would do well to familiarize yourself with all types of games. You never know whether you will end up at a company that only makes role-playing games or one that wants you to work on their new racing game. The more you know, the more opportunities you will have.

The first chapter of this book offers an overview of the industry, explains how games are made, and includes a brief history explaining how computer games have evolved so quickly in such a short time. This is a good foundation for the rest of the book, which is largely divided by job categories, including plenty of tips and pointers from industry insiders. Lastly, there are several appendices with tons of quick reference material for your convenience.

Making a computer game is a team project. Because today's games are so complicated, the notion of a programmer working alone in his or her garage is an outdated one. You will be part of a large team, so understanding the tasks of each member of the group is increasingly useful.

After reading this book, you will want to follow up with some of the suggested reading material for more information on a specific topic. Keep up with industry news and happenings on some of the recommended Web sites. The computer game business moves pretty fast: there are always new games coming out, the capabilities for personal computers (PCs) are always expanding, and, as the popularity of the PlayStation 2, Xbox, and GameCube approach maturity, be on the lookout for the next revolution in console models.

Creating computer games is a competitive job. Once you have finished this book, the next time someone scoffs at your suggestion of making games for a living, you will be able to tell them how much effort really goes into every single minute of entertainment.

CHAPTER 1

FROM *SPACEWAR* TO *THE SIMS*

Some computer games have a cast of characters who wander through cities, go to work, exchange goods and services, and even come into conflict with one another. This might not sound very remarkable, except for the fact that many of the citizens of these cities have human attributes. Take, for example, the characters in one of today's hottest-selling games, *The Sims*. Designed by Will Wright, *The Sims* is the computer gamers' answer to reality television. It is a quirky game of interactive play where characters earn money, leave home, and even occasionally become famous in their virtual world. In fact, since the game hit the marketplace, it has gone on to sell more than 9 million copies, according to a 2002 article in the *Los Angeles Times*.

What is unique about *Sims* players, however, is that they are mostly female. Yet another odd fact about the virtual *Sim* city, at least the online version called Alphaville, is that your characters continue to interact while you are offline. Players from all over the world can catch up with the goings-on in Alphaville before signing on and playing another round. This interactivity between strangers is yet another way that the current world of gaming has reached a new level of excitement.

Today's gamers can also interact as elves, dwarves, and other creatures from fantasy worlds. Some are Wookies and droids from *Star Wars*, while others even revisit the major battles of the Second World War, complete with authentic-looking vehicles and weapons. What is amazing is that these people are united via their computers and computer game consoles to play games that bring them together in virtual reality.

Thanks to the success of games such as *EverQuest*, *Star Wars Galaxies, World War II Online*, and *The Sims*, you can actually take part in grand adventures with thousands of players in a virtual gaming world. Even when you log off, this "world" continues. Your character or online persona remains intact with all the progress or objects picked up during the last game. In fact, some of these games have become so popular that people have bought and sold their online positions in the real world.

Today it takes large teams of individuals to design computer games and keep them running. Despite a common misconception, computer games aren't just a distraction to teenage boys and slackers. With annual revenues that rival the United States' film industry, creating successful computer games has become a big business, drawing the attention of Sony and Microsoft, who now fight for dominance in the market. With each of these companies also taking their respective computer game console systems online, it is almost certain that this form of electronic entertainment won't be disappearing anytime soon.

The computer game industry has grown very quickly over the past few years, and that growth spells jobs for those with skills and talent. According to the U.S.

Department of Labor, the growth of software publishing will likely expand by about 68 percent between 2002 and 2012, making it the fastest-growing industry in the country. There is, however, much more to working with computer games than just playing them (although that's a good perk).

Yes, playing games is necessary to test them (a process that checks to ensure every feature in the game works), but designing a computer game requires more than a keen intuition and fast fingers. Testing games is only one part of the process.

Even game reviewers, people who play and review games so readers can decide if the games are worth purchasing, admit that playing is only a small part of the process. It is also important, says Andrew Reiner, executive editor at *Game Informer* magazine, that you know the specific audience for individual games as well as how the industry has changed. "You have to know the history of computer games," Reiner explains. "That's the thing gamers are looking for; you need to know the facts."

A HISTORY OF THE COMPUTER GAME UNIVERSE

The very first computer game was actually programmed by a college student at the Massachusetts Institute of Technology (MIT) in 1961. An avid fan of science fiction, Steve Russell spent 200 computer hours over the course of six months to develop a simple 2-D game that he called *Spacewar*. Using toggle switches on some of the first personal computers, players would control the speed and direction of their spaceship, while another switch let them fire torpedoes at each other. Although it wasn't immediately available to the public, a later version of Russell's creation would eventually make it to the home in 1972 as a game called *Computer Space*.

It was immediately clear that computer games were a different form of entertainment from anything else. When you read a book, watch a movie, or listen to a CD, your experience is passive, that is, all the information flows one way: toward you. You have no input in what is on the page or screen. Computer games, however, are interactive. Information flows both ways. The screen shows a situation and the viewer controls what happens next. You have the ability to control the experience.

The first successful computer game was *Pong*. This was a defining moment for the gaming industry, since *Pong* was the first game that was embraced by the masses. *Pong* was essentially a simple, electronic form of tennis. Each player controlled a white line on a black screen (the paddle) and hit a white blip (the ball) until someone missed. *Pong* became the game that launched the arcade craze that eventually led to the development in 1975 of the home computer game console.

Atari founder Nolan Bushnell brought *Pong* to Sears Roebuck that same year, and it became the first "at home" version of the same type of entertainment that until then was only found in arcades. Less than two years later, Atari would introduce its home computer system known as the 2600.

These early years saw continued development of coin-operated arcade games for Atari with hit titles such as *Asteroids, Space Invaders*, and *Centipede*, but the American designers soon faced stiff competition from Japan. The most formidable of these Japanese imports was called *Pac-Man*, a simple game that gobbled up quarters almost as fast as the yellow character ate up balls of light. Not only was *Pac-Man* a hit in American arcades, it also spawned a slew of merchandise and its own animated cartoon that began showing on Saturday mornings.

Soon Bushnell's original system brought the arcade into the living room by introducing home versions of arcade blockbusters such as *Pac-Man, Tempest*, and *Space Invaders*. You didn't need quarters anymore, just a television to plug in the game console. Bushnell sold Atari in 1978 to Warner Communications, and the company went head-to-head with another home system, Intellivision, manufactured by Mattel. Thus the first computer game console war was started, a battle that continues today, though the names have changed.

Playing the games at home would also lead to two very significant events for the industry. First, while Atari and Mattel each made their own games exclusively for their individual home systems, other companies began to create original titles for at-home use. These companies were called third-party developers and their games were published to work on both systems. One of these developers was a Japanese company named Nintendo, a corporation that began as a playing card manufacturer. Nintendo has since become one of the largest players in the computer game industry. More important, Nintendo almost single-handedly rescued the future of computer games.

The second significant event is known today simply as "the crash." The arcade business began to decline in the early 1980s, and when Atari released its follow-up home system in 1982, the 5200, it was met by little enthusiasm. Warner Communications sold Atari in 1984. At the time, it seemed as though home computer games might be a passing fad.

A PLUMBER MAKES A HOUSE CALL

The crash in the early 1980s left unsold game cartridges to gather dust in warehouses across the United States. After Atari racked up huge losses, most companies steered away from reentering the console computer game market.

That is, except Nintendo. A Japanese company with more than 100 years of history, Nintendo single-handedly rescued the future of computer games. The developer's star designer, Shigeru Miyamoto, resurrected a character from his arcade hit *Donkey Kong*, and created it as a game that was shipped with Nintendo's new home system released in Japan called Famicom (Family Computer). Nintendo even approached Atari about releasing the system in America, but poor sales of the 5200, as well as plans for a new 7200 system, persuaded the Americans to back out of the deal. Nintendo brought the system to the United States instead, but promoted it as a toy rather than a computer system. The game that was included in the package, *Super Mario Brothers*, gave Nintendo a hit at the end of 1985. The popularity of the Nintendo Entertainment System (NES) fueled long lines at stores during the holiday season and throughout 1986.

Super Mario Brothers captivated a whole new generation of gamers. The game's hero, Mario, was a plumber who braved all sorts of obstacles and monsters to rescue a princess. *Super Mario Brothers* contained tons of secrets such as warp zones to take the player to different levels, and invisible blocks that would yield rewards to inquisitive gamers. It was so popular, in fact, that there weren't many kids who didn't get the NES as a present or play the game at a friend's house. Mario had saved the day for home console systems.

But gaming in other forms was far from dead during this time. While cartridges of Atari, Intellivision, and other systems languished on store shelves, this period remained golden for computer games. That said, it was also a time when the first wave of piracy, the illegal copying of games, would nearly cripple the entire industry.

PERSONAL COMPUTERS

The first personal computers were not especially user-friendly, but that changed with the introduction of another new system called the Commodore 64. The Commodore was powerful for its day, and it featured decent sound and graphics. It was also especially easy to program. Still, the Commodore wasn't the only personal computer (PC) in town. The Apple II, TRS Color Computer, and even IBM's PC were also being sold to gamers. The trouble was that most games were not sold, but were instead copied and traded among gaming fans.

Despite the impact of piracy, the demand for computer games launched several companies including Electronic Arts and Activision, both of which are still active in the industry. The older systems gradually failed to keep pace, and by the early 1990s, only two computer systems remained: IBM's PC and Apple's Mac—the same two choices of computers today. The PC would eventually dominate the home computer market because IBM offered a license and allowed other manufacturers to market clones. Today, IBM has essentially left the PC market, but the platform remains a favorite for gamers thanks to two other developments.

The first was the introduction of the CD-ROM drive. This invention meant that computer games could have more advanced sound and more realistic graphics. Because the CD-ROM itself acts as a "key" to run the software, its invention solved many problems with software piracy. More important, the introduction of Windows 95 meant that PC game developers would have a single standard system on which to run their programs. Computer games were now on par with console games. There continued to be "system requirements," but Windows 95, as well as later versions of Windows software, made the development process much easier. Computer gaming now existed side-by-side on computer game consoles that connected to a television, and those games that were played only on a home computer.

Since the NES system restored the computer game market, it wasn't long before competition sprung up again and a new wave of console wars began. Sega, which rivaled Nintendo in the computer arcades, arrived in the home during the late 1980s with the Sega Genesis machine. Consumer electronics giant Sony began the next revolution with its first console in 1995. Ironically, Sony had previously entered a partnership with Nintendo in the early 1990s to develop a CD-ROM drive for the Super-NES system, but

Nintendo strayed from the deal. Sony decided to take them head on by designing its own console. The result, the PlayStation, would go on to become the best-selling computer game console system ever. Today, nearly one in every three American households owns a PlayStation system.

Success was not as universal for every hardware manufacturer, however. The first company to give Nintendo a run for the money was also the first to exit the computer game hardware arena. After disappointing sales of its Saturn and Dreamcast systems, Sega made the transition to become a third-party game developer and publisher. In recent years, Sega has done quite well building its brand with a group of critically acclaimed sports games. For many longtime Sega fans, it is still interesting to see Sega's popular characters on their former rivals' systems.

The latest console war saw a new competitor enter the fray. Software giant Microsoft, best known for creating the Windows operating system, released its well-received Xbox system in 2001, just days before Nintendo's launch of its new GameCube. The Xbox quickly grabbed the number two spot behind Sony's PlayStation 2.

THEN AND NOW

Computer gaming started in obscurity, but now, more than forty years later, almost everyone is familiar with gaming. In fact, contrary to the usual stereotype that computer games are only played by teenagers, they are actually enjoyed by people of all ages. Recent annual sales suggest that gaming is becoming a bigger form of family entertainment than even going to the movies. With more than $10 billion in revenue for the past five years, computer games are truly appealing to a lot of players.

According to the ESA, the trade organization for the computer game industry, 50 percent of all Americans over the age of six have played some type of computer game.

The average age of gamers is twenty-nine, and 39 percent of gamers are women. The year 2002 saw more than 221 million computers and computer games sold, nearly two for every household in America.

"Games are extremely popular across all ages, especially those between two and thirty-five," emphasizes Doug Lowenstein, president of the ESA, who stresses that games remain a social activity. "There is some evidence that computer games are drawing people away from television viewing. ESA research has found that the vast majority of people who play games do so with friends and family."

Since those early days of *Spacewar*, computer games have continued to evolve. One fact that remains true, however, is that this form of entertainment remains interactive. Unlike television, music, or even books, people aren't only watching or listening, but are reacting to the games they play. Computer games can either be a shared experience or something done completely alone, depending on their design. Most of today's games are being designed with both single-player and multiplayer modes that allow gamers to play with or against other people thousands of miles away.

The very first game to attract mass audiences, *Pong*, was designed entirely as a two-player game. Although it was simple, popular, and designed and programmed by one person, *Pong* brought people together.

Today's games are still bringing people together, but instead of being created by individuals, even the simplest games require a team. While there is no one formula, most teams include a producer to oversee the process, programmers to write the actual code that makes the game run, designers to create its visual appearance, graphic artists to create its artwork, and sound designers to provide its music and sound effects. While Steve Russell spent months programming *Spacewar*, some of today's games take thousands of hours and more than a year to get right. A well-designed game that transports the player to a world that is unique and believable can take months or even years to create.

FROM PITCH TO PRODUCT

To help you understand how a computer game goes from an idea on paper to an actual game on the store shelves, let's examine the process. First, a group of ten to fifteen people, often called the development team, consider ideas, a process usually referred to as brainstorming. A publishing company approves an idea and provides financing. The development team then creates the game from scratch, after which the publishing company takes over and distributes the game to stores. Marketers create a publicity campaign to ensure that the public knows about the game, and then consumers buy the game. This process is a generalized way of looking at what takes a game from an idea on a napkin to the rack at Best Buy. It is not the only method, but it is the most common one.

Let's start with the basics. Computer games can be played in a variety of ways. They run on platforms, machines, or hardware that have the capability to run game software. Currently, you can play games on the following platforms: the PC, a console (PlayStation 2 by Sony, Xbox by Microsoft, GameCube by Nintendo), coin-operated arcade machines (found outside the home), handheld devices (Game Boy Advanced by Nintendo and N-Gage by Nokia), and portable devices such as mobile phones, personal data assistants (PDAs), and pocket PCs.

The console business is the biggest segment of the industry. Its growth is aided by the fact that you can do so much more on them than ever before. A PC is designed to perform a variety of functions, with gaming only playing a part of the mix. Current consoles are designed specifically to play games, but this is also changing. Today's generation of consoles is also able to access the Internet (principally to download bonus content and play online against people who live thousands of miles away). The Xbox and PlayStation 2 can even be connected to a PC and serve as a media center to run computer, audio, and picture files on the TV and home stereo system. Console systems are not just for games anymore.

Game-makers can be divided into two groups of people. The folks who create, design, and program games are called developers. The other group is made up of publishers who finance, manufacture, market, and distribute the games. Because games cost a lot of money to make, developers will often look to a partnering publisher for the monetary backing to create a finished product. The publisher creates all of the packaging materials for the game (the box, the artwork on the box, the instruction manual), designs and purchases ads on television, on the Internet, and in magazines, and then gets the game to retailers either directly or through a distributor.

That hot-selling game that you picked up at Best Buy last week has probably been in development for the last year or longer. It likely began as a simple idea from an individual or two, and then, after a bit of brainstorming with others, a rough outline came together. From there, the game developer started to put the wheels in motion and created a series of business plans, outlines, and concept sketches.

Because creating a game takes a large team, plenty of money to support the salaries of the creative staff is needed. This requires an investment in time and energy on the part of the game development studio—the people who will make the game—and an investment of money from a game publisher. Many larger publishers such as Microsoft, Electronic Arts, and Sony have their very own game studios. This is called in-house development, but these same companies also listen to ideas from independently owned game developers, or third-party developers, because they are not owned or operated by the publisher.

Whether the game developer is in-house or a third-party company, the process usually remains the same. The publisher will want to see pitches and feel confident that the game will succeed. A game that doesn't sell well doesn't make any money, so publishers need to feel comfortable that a game will sell well enough to make a return on the initial investment.

After a publisher agrees to finance a game, the team begins the development process. The game developer needs to design all the art, create the plot, code the software to make it work, and put in the sound and other effects. When all of this is finished, the game's "balance" is tested by game testers. It is important that the game is easy to win but still offers a challenge to players. Testers need to make sure the game works well and that it doesn't crash because of software bugs or other glitches. When all of this is done, the game's publisher gets the software code and releases it to stores, much such as a record company does with a CD.

Before a game arrives in stores, a marketing team works to make sure that consumers know about it. This involves sending copies to computer game reviewers at magazines, preparing television ad campaigns, placing ads in magazines, and preparing contests and other promotions to attract attention. Many computer games for the PC have downloadable levels so you can try a mission or part of the game before buying it. All of this is done to attract sales.

In the end, if the game is good and everyone has done his or her job properly, the title should be a hit. Still, things can go wrong. The game might have some problems, causing it to crash, or it is too easy and people are not challenged by it. Unfortunately, there is no clear-cut formula to making a successful computer game.

At the end of the day, working to make a best-selling game can be especially rewarding. It requires long hours, often spent in front of a computer, to get everything right. However, when it comes together, making a game can provide something that will delight people and offer a unique and interactive form of entertainment.

A VIEW FROM THE INSIDE

Working in the computer game industry is a unique experience. Unlike the cubicle farms of many offices that consist of rows of uniform work environments, the game world often takes a different approach. One such example is Insomniac Games' 18,000 square feet (1,672 sq. meters) of office space at the top of a building in Burbank, California, where "no cubicles" is the rule. Ted Price founded the company in 1994, and Insomniac has since spawned hits such as the *Ratchet & Clank* and *Spyro the Dragon* series.

Working at Insomniac has its perks. A masseuse comes in once a week, and employees order their own desks and chairs. The huge employee kitchen is stocked with food, soft drinks, and bottled water.

Everyone has a PlayStation 2 at his or her desk. "Part of our jobs as game makers is to play games," Price explains. Many employees clutter their shelves with action figures and other toys. "Hey, we're not working on accounting software," Price said. "We're working on games."

In between numerous cardboard standees of popular movie characters, people often crash on couches during crunch time, or wind down on some of the old consoles around the office, such as the Sega Genesis. "The Ping-Pong table in the old office got out of hand," Price explains. The only thing missing, he says, is a small movie theater. "This is a place where people can feel comfortable. I like to see people enjoy what they do."

When the Insomniacs have had enough of their wild office, they go on field trips to Disneyland, or to wildlife reserves. But why leave the complex? In addition to a gym inside the building, the outside grounds boast a volleyball court, a mini putting green, and a basketball half-court. If you're intrigued, check out Insomniac's Web site to see if the company is hiring (http://www.insomniacgames.com).

CHAPTER 2

BREAKING IN

The days of a programmer working alone in his or her garage to create a groundbreaking computer game are over. These days, contemporary developers divide the production strategy of computer game design into several teams of people.

A producer oversees the entire project. He or she organizes all the production teams and sets the game's budget and various deadlines. The producer ensures that every team member is doing what he or she is assigned to do, and that the game's development remains on schedule.

The role of the design team is to shape the game itself. Designers create the design document, which details everything about the proposed game: the plot, the characters, the goals, and the obstacles. They will physically create each level of the game based on the software the programmers have developed.

The programming team builds the "guts" of the game. Programmers write lines of computer code that outline specific instructions for the computer or game console. Visual artists create the look of the game: they decide how the characters should appear, what the game's environments look like, and paint mock-ups of all the scenes, props, and vehicles—every object that will eventually appear in a finished game. A special type of artist called an animator will work on getting these characters and objects to move the way the designers want them to in order to advance the game to higher levels of play.

Sound designers work on the game's audio elements, which can involve recording anything from screeching car tires to a crying baby. Just as it is strange to watch a movie without sound, audio adds another important effect to any computer game. Sound designers work on special effects (such as gunshots), character dialogue, and music.

The game tester is the final member of the production team. The game tester plays every aspect of the game at each level (beginner through advanced) again and again to make sure there are not any computer code errors, which are called bugs. In fact, many programmers often begin their careers as game testers. This is one of the only entry-level positions where it is possible to learn the entire process of game design from the ground up. Today, entering the field as a game tester is considered one of the best ways to get your foot in the door.

Other, less direct jobs in the computer game industry include the marketers who set the strategy to sell the game, public relations personnel who promote and advertise a finished game, and journalists who write articles and reviews about games.

GETTING STARTED

The first qualification for getting a job in the computer game industry is an obvious one. You should love games! Simply enjoying the act of playing games (eventually leading to constructing and deconstructing the computer code behind them) and having an avid and curious mind are among the most important characteristics of a successful career in the industry. For game testers, the hours are long and the pay is minimal. If you don't love playing games, you'll just be unhappy. Simply put, today's top companies want people who are passionate about computer gaming.

While colleges have offered degrees in computer programming and animation for some time, they are now beginning to tailor certain courses specifically toward game development. Two schools in particular, DigiPen in Washington State, and Full Sail in Florida, have garnered reputations as colleges specifically geared toward computer game programming and design. DigiPen's chief operating officer, Jason Chu, recommends having at least a 2.5 grade point average (GPA) in high school with a 3.0 in classes such as algebra, geometry, trigonometry, and precalculus to improve your chances of gaining admittance to the specialty college. "Nintendo informed us that the time they spent in getting the DigiPen graduates up to speed to program on the GameCube was two weeks, whereas the average for others is twelve to eighteen months," Chu said in a recent interview. A typical day at DigiPen includes six hours of classes and seven hours of lab time. DigiPen also offers two-week summer workshops for middle school and high school students in video game programming, computer animation, and robotics. Samples of student projects are available at http://www.digipen.com/programs/gallery.

But getting your foot in the door at a popular gaming company such as Activision or Electronic Arts requires more than the desire to play games. Even high school graduates entering college (and searching for that perfect summer job) are required to "sell" themselves. To do so, you'll need to create a neat, professional résumé. If possible, ask a guidance counselor or English teacher to proofread it for you. He or she may have suggestions on how to improve the document by catching errors you might have missed.

Even so, your résumé will most likely not be loaded with job references. Since computer game companies are team-oriented, think about experiences you may have had where you were an active member of a group. Have you

Games Ahead 2K4

3D Computer Animation: Level One — $845

3D Computer Animation and special effects are used in many of today's computer/video games and Hollywood movies. This workshop is designed to give high school students an introduction to the concepts and the process of creating a 3D computer animation. Students will also be taught about the importance of strong traditional art skills when using this technology as a production tool. Some of the topics presented include:

- Overview of the 3D computer animation industry
- Basic modeling techniques
- Creation of materials & texture maps
- Basic lighting techniques
- Basic camera manipulation
- Hierarchy linking
- Basic keyframing techniques
- Rendering

DigiPen Institute of
game development
workshop series d
of all experience le
programming and
at the DigiPen ca
the two-week wor
considering a seriou

The DigiPen Institute of Technology, located near Seattle, Washington, is one of the nation's leading facilities for college-level instruction in the field of computer game design and programming. In addition, it also offers summer workshops to qualified high school and middle school students who have demonstrated an interest in computer game design. Programs include classes in animation, computer programming, and robotics.

organized a club at school? Ever been the captain of a sports team? Have you worked on the school newspaper with a staff? This information demonstrates that you have experience working in a team environment, meeting deadlines, and solving problems. Also, it is just as important that you list any aptitude you may have in various software programs. For entry-level positions, the ability to use a word processing program (such as Microsoft Word), a spreadsheet program (such as Excel), an e-mail program (such as Outlook), and a database is a huge plus. Familiarity with art programs (such as Adobe Photoshop or Adobe Illustrator) or animation software (such as 3D Studio Max) is also a highly marketable bonus.

NETWORKING

You may have heard of the saying, "It's not what you know, it's who you know." That is especially true in the game industry. It always helps to know someone on the inside. That may not sound fair, but look at the situation from the company's perspective: a game studio has a tightly knit stable of employees who work long hours for a shared goal. Chemistry between its employees is very important. This philosophy often remains true during the search for a new hire. For example, an existing employee might say, "Well, my friend John is looking for a job and he's extremely reliable." It's quite possible that the company would much rather prefer to interview John, a person one of its employees recommends, rather than go through another stack of anonymous résumés. What do you do if you don't have a contact such as this? Begin networking early. Attend industry conferences and approach people from companies that capture your interest. This is another way to spread your résumé. If you live outside a major city and traveling to conferences is difficult, try a virtual visit: go to a company's message board and examine its human resources information. Many companies now have message boards with specific information about available jobs and internships. Join the group and become an active member of its community by contributing to the forum. This is another kind of networking.

GETTING NOTICED

Another terrific way to demonstrate hands-on programming knowledge is to show potential employers any programs that you have written or modified. Most new programmers don't create entire games anymore. Creating games today requires teams of people working thousands of hours and spending hundreds of thousands (if not millions) of dollars.

Nearly all computer game publishers have engaging and interactive Web sites, such as this one at http://www.activision.com. The Internet is where gaming enthusiasts can find information about upcoming releases, request online support, download trial games and extras, and peruse community bulletin boards. These semi-private forums are often where like-minded people can learn about the company's job and internship openings, upcoming seminars, and the latest news as it relates to gaming.

No one expects you to have made an entire game on the caliber of *Doom 3*. On the other hand, perhaps you've created a cool new program that renders water ripples better than anything else on the market. Or maybe it's a program that replicates fire effects, simulates clouds, or mimics certain body movements in an improved way. All of these ideas are great supplements to your résumé. Burn a CD-ROM and send it along, too. This is your "demo" (demonstration) disc and your best tool to break into the industry.

Developing a new program, however, is only one option. Many games include design tools that enable ambitious fans to modify or even create from scratch their own levels and missions that may be played in that game. This is a great opportunity for the novice, because all the tools are already in front of you. Quality counts more than quantity, so it is better to create one or two incredible levels, rather than a bunch of mediocre changes. You should then make the levels available on community forums to get feedback from other players. If they are well received, include them on a CD-ROM with your résumé. Remember to work on a popular, contemporary game. For instance, don't create a new level for *Unreal Tournament 2003*, when you ought to be working on its 2005 release.

Another, more ambitious, option is to create a mod. A "mod" (modification) takes an existing game and alters significant parts to produce a new gaming experience. Creating a new game from scratch requires an exhaustive amount of time and resources, but a smaller team working with an existing game's software code can actually create a top-notch mod that gains attention. "Publishers are looking for people to design levels," says Billy Pidgeon, a computer game industry analyst and former executive producer at Acclaim Entertainment, in a recent interview. "You could eventually get a job [by creating a mod]." Some mod-making software is available at several Web sites such as http://www.valvesoftware.com/hlsdk.htm, and http://www.swissquake.ch/chumbalum-soft/ms3d/download.html.

Get the Word Out

While you don't need to be an expert programmer to create a decent mod, it won't help you at all if you can't circulate it. If you've created an excellent new character for an existing game, or changed the game in a way that makes it more exciting or competitive, you'll want to let more people in on your talent than your immediate circle of friends. The secret is networking. According to Acclaim's producer, Brandon Fish, knowing even one person who is already employed in the industry is a great start:

It can help to find a friend who's already inside. A lot of times publishers need testers, even if it's just temporary. It gets your foot in the door. You meet people and you learn the process [of making a game from start to finish]. It's not necessarily playing games all day like a lot of people seem to think.

It can help to go to industry events. Things like GDC [Game Developers Conference] turn out to be people just handing out their résumés. Some of the people are out of work and some are people trying to get in. It is easy to get lost in the shuffle; you want to make sure your stuff stands out. You want to make sure you have a well-written, one-page résumé. If you're inexperienced, make sure you list your education and show your work. Some openings [require] three to five years' experience, so you're going to have to blow people away.

One of the biggest success stories is *Counter-Strike*, a user-created mod that began as a multiplayer mode for the groundbreaking game *Half Life*. This mod, which pits terrorists against counterterrorist Special Forces, even surpassed the original game's popularity. It was eventually picked up by the publisher of *Half Life* and released commercially before spawning a full-blown sequel.

Another example is *Desert Combat*. Based on *Battlefield 1942*, a World War II multiplayer simulation in which Allied players take on a team of Axis players, *Desert Combat* took the game to the present, where helicopters and Humvees replace propeller planes and tanks. Each of these mods achieved equal, if not more, popularity than the games they improved upon.

Creating a mod requires a group of dedicated people and a considerable amount of time. Community forums, such as http://www.planethalflife.com/modcentral, are good places to find like-minded people if your friends aren't up to the task. A finished, polished mod is a great tool when searching for job opportunities. Invite the game's developers to try it out. Send them demo CDs. Get the word out about your ideas on message boards. Computer game publishers usually create Web sites and community forums for their current games. This is a good place to start.

According to Brandon Fish, Acclaim Studio's producer, creating a mod is among the most effective steps for entering the business.

If you can create a mod, that helps tremendously. But it's got to be high quality. Nobody's going to look at a mod that is [poorly designed]. [This process usually requires] a full team. If you can get together a bunch of guys, like the guys [who] made Counter-Strike *or* Half Life, *if you can be lucky enough to create something that's high quality; [something] you'd be proud to show somebody. [It is helpful to create] anything that you can show to a studio; to show that you're committed to a project. If you don't have a team to work with and you're interested in game design, work on a [single] level.*

If you haven't guessed by now, community forums are excellent places to get involved. Yet another way in which becoming a member of a community forum pays a great dividend is beta testing. A beta version of a game is one that runs but still has a few bugs that the developer and publisher want eliminated before the game is released. Beta testers consist of a small group of industry insiders, press reporters, and fans. Try to get yourself on this list. You'll have to play the game, report any bugs you encounter, and provide feedback on how well or poorly the game's features ran. If you can communicate clearly, you may very well find yourself on the inside track to getting a paid tester position. It's also a great way to meet people in the industry. Do remember to explain your points carefully, using reason and arguments where appropriate. Use constructive criticism. Be polite, informative, and helpful.

THE INTERVIEW

Everyone knows that you have to be well prepared for any job interview, but what does this mean? Employers expect prospective employees to dress neatly, and to be well groomed. This includes a clean-shaven face for men, conservative hairstyles for women, and manicured hands. Depending on the company's philosophy, you might want to dress conservatively. Above all, keep your attire simple. Finally, wear a minimal amount of jewelry, accessories, and makeup.

Being prepared also means carrying a pen and several copies of your résumé on clean, white (or light-colored) paper. Think about the interview beforehand, and imagine questions that might come up during the conversation. What's your favorite game and why? What's your least favorite game and why? What were the last three or four games you played? The interviewer doesn't care if *Doom* or *Unreal Tournament* is your favorite game. He or she cares about why it's your favorite game. He or she wants to know whether you can clearly explain your position, give reasons for your choice, and support your answer. Quite simply, he or she wants to know whether you can communicate clearly.

If people in the computer game business communicated poorly, it would take a much longer time to create solid games. As with any business, time is money. With thousands—or millions—of dollars in development, marketing, and advertising at stake, interviewers want to know whether you are able to express your opinions effectively without wasting time.

However, there are two sides to communication. Companies also want to know that potential employees can listen as well as speak. Many interviewees, therefore, include a written essay. This serves two purposes: first, it is yet another opportunity for you to demonstrate how well you can communicate. Second, it is a chance to show that you can listen and follow directions. Don't go off on a wild tangent. Just relax and answer the questions that are asked of you. Most likely, it will be something like "Describe various problems in a recent computer game you played and how you would like to see them corrected."

"HOW I GOT MY START. . ."

Brandon Fish, Producer, Acclaim Studios

When I was in college, all I did was play computer games. I got started working for a Web site devoted to the game Quake. *That got me to know a few people in the industry so I made a few* Quake *maps. After school, I sent demo CDs around. I had already signed on to do a map for* Sin *(without compensation, but it was a nice attribute on my résumé). I got my first paying gig working on a map for the multiplayer game* Kingpin. *High Voltage [then] hired me as an assistant producer.*

David Perry, Founder, Shiny Entertainment

[When] I was in high school, I sat down and played around with a computer and wrote some terrible programs. I was amazed that I got them printed in some magazines." [Note: *In the early 1980s, games were simple enough that the entire program could be printed line by line in a magazine. Readers would type the program very carefully into their computers to play it. One tiny mistake would often prevent*

Careers in the Computer Game Industry

---

the program from running.] I got started making games on the Timex Sinclair ZX81, that was over twenty years ago. That little machine only had 1K of RAM. Today a standard PC comes with over 256K. That was so little memory back then, that when you needed to add another line of program, you had to delete something else to make room! The good news was, however, that this little machine had a keyboard (instead of a joystick), and so while many console gamers could only play games, people with the little ZX81 were able to get their programming careers started. I was one of those lucky people.

Sean Sharp, QA (Quality Assurance Tester) and Project Lead, Acclaim Entertainment

My story's a little different than most. My friend, Rob, was writing for his college newspaper and got passes for [the] Electronics Entertainment Expo [E3] in Atlanta in 1998. There was a cover girl for an Acclaim game, Forsaken. It turns out Rob had grown up with her. We went with her to the Sega party, met somebody in public relations from Acclaim, and I got a job interview.

Kyle Hudson, Manager of Product Testing, Nintendo

My best friend was actually working at Nintendo while we were in college, and I needed a job. He mentioned to me that he was able to play games while answering the phones. I couldn't believe it, so I went to the temp agency and let them know that I wanted to work at Nintendo. Well, I got the job, but they put me on a production line in their production department. It was fine, but I wanted to be on the phones playing games. I ended up going back to the agency and they transferred me to the consumer service department so I could play games and answer phones!

Dan Amrich, Senior Editor, *GamePro* magazine

> *I started out doing music reviews straight out of college, and my editor at* Critics' Choice *asked if I would be interested in doing a few games. That turned into a three-year stint as the senior games' editor, during which I wrote about 300 reviews [without compensation]. I got to keep the games I reviewed, and I built up a huge body of work as well as a good reputation as a solid freelancer. My day job was at* Guitar World *magazine, which also had a few sister publications involving computer games, so I got print and online experience simultaneously. I kept setting goals for bigger and better freelance gigs while doing* Critics' Choice *and eventually switched over to [writing about] games full-time. A lot of people hear that I worked three years for free and freak out, but that's what I felt it took to get where I wanted to be. The work is fun, but it's a competitive field. Nothing good comes easy.*

Matt Schlosberg, Public Relations Manager, Acclaim Entertainment

> *I've always been into games. I studied broadcast news and wanted to be an anchorman, but I realized it wasn't for me. I wanted to be behind the scenes. I gave public relations a shot and enjoyed it. Even when you have a bad day, you have to say to yourself, "Hey, I work on computer games, not tax software."*

Remember, computer games are created by teams of dedicated people who work hard to achieve their collective goals of creating the best possible games. While certain individuals may work on some tasks alone, at the end of the day, every member of the team must be able to communicate clearly to the others what is needed or how the task is progressing.

CHAPTER 3

THE ROLE OF GAME TESTERS

This entry-level job might be the most misunderstood position in the entire computer game industry. The common misconception about the role of game testers is that they play games for eight hours a day. Actually, nothing could be further from the truth. A position as a game tester is hard work, often with little glory. However, there is perhaps no better or more common way to break into the industry.

Put any ideas about playing games out of your head for a moment. There is much more to the game tester position than that. Each day, the project lead (also called the lead tester or quality assurance lead) will give you a game and specific instructions about what you are searching for in that game. Estimating the quality of a particular game is usually not determined by playing it from beginning to end. The project lead has a database of all the game's bugs and its features that need to be checked for specific changes or modifications. He or she will control the group of QA testers and let each one know what he or she is to report about during game play. Anytime any QA testers encounter a bug, they write a bug report, which is entered into a database by someone with more experience. Over time, QA testers will see how bugs are rewritten and formatted. Once QA testers have significant experience, they will enter the changes directly into a template. This information is then uploaded directly into the larger computer database and reviewed by the project lead.

There are perks to being in the QA department. Many companies bring their testers with them to Los Angeles for the Electronics Entertainment Expo (E3) each year, which showcases games that will hit the shelves the following year. When a new computer game system comes out, testers will be able to get hands-on playing time well before the public does.

There's also a downside to quality testing: playing game after game can become tedious. "You get so sick of the game that you just don't want to see it anymore," says Sean Sharp, QA project lead at Acclaim Entertainment. At the tail end of any game's development cycle, when it is almost out the door, QA testers spend a lot of the day just trying to get a weird anomaly to occur, a phase in the process often referred to as collision testing. "Collision testing is pretty monotonous," Sharp adds. Collision testing necessitates trying every move imaginable, something that can take many hours. Stretching your legs helps, but a lot of break rooms at computer game companies have stand-up arcade machines and console games from rival companies. Sometimes QA testers even opt to play games during their break and lunch times!

Testing is vital to ensure that the games are released without any anomalies or bugs that would impair the player's enjoyment or ability to complete the game. "Without testing the games, there would be a lot of unhappy gamers," says Kyle Hudson, manager of product testing at Nintendo. "[QA] testers are doing more than just playing; they are trying different things that maybe the game wasn't programmed for, or they are trying steps out of sequence. If a QA tester is able to get a bug to occur, then he or she will try to duplicate that bug to help provide information in a detailed written description." This description usually details exactly how he or she was able to get the bug to occur. According to Kyle Hudson, manager of product testing at Nintendo, many QA testers have to work together to locate various bugs. "Many times a tester will find an issue and if he or she is unable to nail down the steps, he or she will ask their other team members if they have any ideas on how to duplicate the issue. They also work together to accomplish specific goals or objectives assigned to them. Both of these examples lead to great teamwork and the feeling of accomplishment."

Quality assurance testers also have the opportunity to confirm that bugs have been fixed, attend meetings, conduct specific quality control tests/procedures, contribute to creative development, and perform balance testing. These other duties bring some variety to the position. The number of QA testers working on a particular game differs from day to day. Depending on the type of game, the deadline and the level of complexity, a QA team can consist of between two to fifteen people.

Another type of QA tester also gets to see a game in its early stage, and this is the beta tester. Beta software is essentially a game or other software that is nearly finished but not quite ready to be released to the public. At this late stage, the game or software is mostly playable, but it still requires a bit more work. Usually unpaid, beta testers are recruited by game companies to play these unfinished games and track their problems. Oftentimes beta testers will have to supply their feedback to the QA department, which will incorporate this information with its own bug reports.

Computer games for the PC require an extra examination called compatibility testing. Unlike a console such as PlayStation 2, each personal computer is a little different. A game designed for a console works for that specific console only. A PC game must run on any variety of PC. Testers must ensure that the game can run on any imaginable configuration of PC. If the game involves an Internet capability, testers must run it on dial-up modems and through high-speed broadband lines.

QUALIFICATIONS

The entry-level position of QA tester is a likely first position for many young people entering the industry. You can improve your chances of landing this gig by taking steps to turn yourself into an ideal candidate. First, have an intimate familiarity with basic computer software programs such as Microsoft Word, Excel, and Outlook. Another huge advantage is having the ability to understand how to use a basic database.

Second, you must be an effective communicator, with excellent verbal and written skills. The ability to understand each person's suggestions and solutions in a fast-paced group environment is crucial. Taking directions, following specific instructions, and meeting deadlines are vital.

Nintendo's Hudson recommends having a high school diploma and working toward a college degree (if not already earned). A QA tester, he says, "should be able to stay focused on the task at hand, communicate effectively through verbal interaction and in writing, sit for long periods of time, have the ability to perform repetitive and monotonous tasks, and be detail oriented." According to Hudson, talented game players have an advantage, but being a hard worker who can think creatively and communicate well is just as important.

Even if you are still in high school, you can look for opportunities in gaming companies for beta testers. This type of game tester is usually done for the PC, because console systems such as PlayStation 2 require special noncommercial versions to play prerelease software. As a beta tester, you'll need to have a fairly fast and powerful computer. A high-speed Internet connection can also help optimize your downloading time. Major publishers will occasionally post notices on their Web sites about public beta tests and offer sign-up information.

Stick to gaming styles that you know well. For example, if you largely play strategy games, don't try to sign up for every action shooter beta test. The QA teams look for experienced gamers in a particular genre, and even if you don't make the cut, you should try to choose seriously.

Testing games in their early stages isn't always the same as playing a finished game. Levels might be shorter, the artwork might be incomplete, and the game might even crash. But most important, if you get the chance to beta test a game and the developers ask for feedback, try to provide as much detailed information as possible. This can make the difference between launching a career and just getting an occasional chance to play a game before it hits store shelves.

Once on staff, the hours for QA testers can be brutal. Acclaim's Sharp recalls one particularly severe crunch time. "From 4 AM to 6 PM, six days a week for two and a half months. The seventh day was usually about five hours just to catch up on things you couldn't get done during the week. We were all toast," says Sharp, who started in the business as a QA tester. He insists that the easiest way to break in is to know someone. "The Electronics Entertainment Expo [E3] is always a great place to start; it's like 'job hunt country,'" he continues. "Every company has human resources representatives there. [Some people] call ahead of time and set up an appointment." Right around the summer, when college semesters are ending, is usually a good time when companies are hiring. Crunch time is in the summer for games coming out in the fall.

Sometimes working as a QA tester at a game developing company differs greatly from the same position at a game publisher, according to Sharp, now a project leader at Acclaim. "Sometimes a studio has a ridiculously small test crew. They might have two people for two projects. Their jobs are just to make sure the game works well enough to send over to the full test crew at the publisher's offices. It takes a while to transfer a game—could take eight hours to burn it. If it doesn't work, then they [have] wasted that eight hours instead of spending one hour to make sure it works. You would do what's called smoke testing where you run through the game from point A to point B the easiest way possible."

As a QA tester for either type of company, the rigorous schedule is commonplace. You have to enjoy working those hours for almost any position in the [gaming] industry. "There are a lot of people who don't make it past thirty [years of age] in this industry," Sharp says. "They move on to something else." As a project lead, Sharp has the luxury of overtime pay, but plenty of testers do not, even though they log the same number of hours. Why do they do it? Their love for the games keeps them going. "A lot [of] people want to see the thing they are working on succeed," Sharp explains. The typical tester is personable, able to work in a confidential and dynamic environment, and is a team player. But if you mind spending hour after hour in front of a computer monitor, it's not the job for you.

A Day in the Life of a Project Leader

For project leaders, daily duties can change from day to day. Although a project leader will work on one project from beginning to end (which could take several months), he or she will have a number of QA testers reporting to him or her each day, each with a separate set of problems and questions. As a project leader, you must manage and update a database that tracks all the bug reports for that title. As problems arise, a project leader contacts the game's producer and informs the company headquarters (such as Sony, Microsoft, or Nintendo) of any significant progress, scheduling problems, and so on. Being a project leader requires a lot of micromanaging as well as top organizational skills.

CAREER GROWTH

Although the QA tester position is an entry-level job, it holds the potential for great advancement for anyone who is dedicated. In essence, as a QA tester you get your feet wet by learning the basics of game development. Testing games is an integral component of that process, but it is only a small part of the larger picture.

To move up the production ladder, be proactive. Don't just do what you have to do and go home. If somebody's asking for added feedback on a project, offer it. Putting in the extra hours can mean the difference when it comes time to promote QA testers to the next level. Always offer to pitch in whenever you can. Not only will you prove yourself a valuable asset to the team, you will also be learning more game-making skills. It's also beneficial to work in a studio with a development team rather than in a company's headquarters. You will have greater access to the tools you would eventually be working with as a game-maker.

As a QA tester, be prepared to start out as an unpaid intern or with a modest salary in the $25,000 to $35,000 range. For many people, the position of QA tester is a path to something else. For example, in Sharp's QA department at Acclaim, the turnover has been great. "We had two guys that left for design positions in Austin [Texas]. Another guy left to be an artist. Another guy left [when he was offered a job as a] game designer. [And still] another left to be a programmer at Sony. We had a few people leave for marketing [jobs]."

CHAPTER 4

COMPUTER GAME DESIGNERS

Anyone thinking of entering the computer game industry with one bright idea should think again. Almost everyone who has played computer games has thought, "Hey, I would love to play a game that had . . ." While it would be great to go to work, call a meeting, and say, "OK, everyone, I've got a great idea for a game," the process is far more complicated. The designer needs more than a good idea. He or she needs to be intimately familiar with all aspects of the production process. Successful designers need to focus on making games that are not only fun, but won't cost too much, or take too much time to create. Computer games are not created in a vacuum. Game publishers such as Microsoft have their own ideas about the types of games they want to produce. Also, console makers such as Sony and Nintendo are demanding specific elements in their games.

Every game begins with a design document that is created by the design team. This is a reference guide to every aspect of the game including its initial concept, sketches of its characters, and the outline of its plot and other features. In its early stages, the design document contains information about the proposed game's structure, such as its various levels of difficulty, what a player should accomplish at each level, and an overall summary of how the game will function. Throughout the process, the design document will develop further. More complete design documents contain concept sketches or drawings on how the characters and environments will look; a script, the dialogue the characters will speak; screen shots, which are still pictures of the actual game; and flowcharts on the movement of the hero throughout the game's plot. It's a lot to manage.

"A design document might call for a big, beefy enemy," says Berenger Fish, lead designer of Acclaim Entertainment. "The artist might say, 'I have some ideas; he'll have a limp.' The designer needs to say, 'No, he can't have a limp. He needs to be fast.' That information should be in the design document. The design document should have a balance between allowing too much creative freedom and not enough. It ought to be able to convey the overall vision while avoiding the dangers of too little or too much detail. In many cases,

During development, visual artists render drawings or paintings of prospective computer game characters, such as this sketch for *Call of Duty* by Activision.

a paragraph explaining where the action takes place, what the conflicts are, and how the plot advances is enough."

Fish continues, "Some ideas are great on paper but not in practice. This was the case when we tried to create a type of targeting system for a game. As it turned out, it wasn't challenging enough. We then had to decide whether to continue working on it or advance the game in a different direction."

According to Will Wright, the creator of the popular series of *Sims* games including *SimCity* and *The Sims*, if the design document isn't specific enough, it might say, "This guy has a shotgun and he's trying to get close to the player. And he can use cover." That's not telling the programmer how the enemy works. How close does he get to the player? What happens if he can't get close enough to the player? Designers have to anticipate any problems that might come up.

The designer must also ensure that the game is fun and challenging for all types of players. Is the game considered too easy to hold a player's attention, or is it too challenging for beginners? The person who takes charge of all these tasks is called the lead designer.

Alex Garden, CEO of Relic Entertainment, knows all about being a lead designer and the difficulties of starting a new project. He founded his company in 1997 after working with Electronic Arts and Radical Entertainment, and went on to create the award-winning real-time strategy game *Homeworld* and its sequel, *Homeworld 2*.

The early part of the design process is fairly basic, explains Garden, "The first meeting is a very early process where we share ideas and are putting together our pitch document, and when we know that one idea might be picked up, we go to the next stage. This is our proof-of-concept stage and where we build the playable content as a prototype. It shows that the game is playable and that it's fun."

Creating a game that is fun to play is important, but a variety of elements and their effectiveness need to be relayed to a potential publisher. "At this early stage we wait to have a go, no-go moment with the publisher. If it's a go, we move forward with what we have," explains Garden. "Then we decide the budget and start to get the team in place—programmers, artists, animators, and sound designers. Once that's done, we go into full production. This is where we begin to build the game from the ground up."

Once the production process begins, a lead designer will direct a team of level designers. Level designers use layout editors (the first program that designers use to build the schematic or flowchart for the game) and other programs to create the structure of the worlds the hero must navigate. A layout or level editor is a tool that allows a designer to quickly place existing elements created by the art department into the game. A designer will go to a menu of objects, select one, and place it in the world. In this fashion, a designer shapes the path of the hero. Perhaps he will put a high wall to block the hero's progress. In this case, the hero must turn to another direction, where the designer has placed another obstacle such as a group of bad guys. Designers also program scripts for nonplayer characters. These scripts are lines of programming code that tell the computer-controlled characters what to do, where to go, and how to behave. Level designers base their work off the design document, which contains an outline and descriptions of each level. Depending on how the lead designer likes to work, level designers may have more or less freedom to do what they want to do when building any level.

The entire production team must have an understanding of the architecture of the game and its tone. This requires a close working relationship. According to Bruce Shelley, senior game designer at Ensemble Studios, everyone's opinion is taken into consideration during production, but the lead designer must manage all the input.

"We value highly the input of everyone in our company," says Shelley, who has worked on the best-selling

Age of Empires series. "We ask all staff to play games in development at least once per week in a monitored test session. For these [test sessions] we usually have a designer or test leader set goals for the test [followed by] a feedback session afterward. We want people with a variety of skills and tastes to be involved. We want our game to appeal to a broad audience, so we feel we must get a broad spectrum of [players] involved."

The designers must filter all this feedback and decide what's most important. One person in the art department might suggest a cartoonlike look for all the characters; another may opt for a grittier, more realistic style. One level designer might want to have the hero plow through a series of bloody fights, while another might prefer that the hero spend more time exploring the world than fighting. Changes are made frequently. This means that a game continually evolves. Shelley stresses that not every complaint and comment means a change is in order. "If design gets into conflict with other crafts—principally programming or art—any decision may be kicked up to the producer for resolution."

In the end, the game must never be monotonous. "You don't want forty jumps in a row," explains Berenger Fish, lead designer at Acclaim Entertainment, where he headed the production of *100 Bullets*, a game based on the popular comic book. Fish broke into the industry by designing levels of *Quake* in his spare time. He stresses the importance of building the tension and drama in a game by drawing a player into its plot. "You want to vary it up: a rest area, an exploration area." A good designer, he adds, is able to step back and look at the big picture: when should a character find a weapon? When should the enemies pop up and how often?

Sometimes designers may need to call upon additional help. While it is the designer who usually creates a game's exposition, or background information that leads the hero to the starting point of the game, a writer or screenwriter may be hired to handle the duties of providing

dialogue or "fleshing out" the story. A writer will work closely with the lead designer to ensure that what he or she is writing matches the intended direction of the game. In some cases, a game development studio will have a staff writer handle these duties instead. It is not all creative writing, however. Technical writing is also necessary for writing the game's manual and transforming notes taken in a meeting into a design document.

QUALIFICATIONS

Many of today's biggest designers started out as gamers, but it obviously takes more than a high score on *Mario* to be a top-notch designer. Bruce Shelley, senior game designer at Ensemble Studios, admits that he even had to stop thinking too much like a player.

> *I have played games for most of my life. I have never stopped being a player, but moving over to being a designer required a lot of new thinking. One key challenge was to think in terms of a broad audience, not just what I want[ed] to play. I think it helped that I was an [average] person and my likes seem to have been shared by many others.*

The creation of a game level or mission is done using a level-editing program. This software will vary depending on the type of game you are creating. The more editors you have used, the better. The level editors for the *Quake*, *Unreal Tournament*, and *Tony Hawk's Pro Skater* games are very popular and are a great place to start. They're very straightforward. These programs provide good practice for learning how to place objects, enemies, and mission objectives in a game environment. Have a friend try out your level, or put the file up on the Internet to get feedback from other players. New designers start out working on levels, so practicing the craft in order to build up a body of sample work is very important to landing your first job.

Some programming knowledge is required to script the actions and reactions of the computer-controlled characters. Knowing the basics of storytelling and suspense is helpful because creating a good level or mission relies on these foundations. A level or mission is a segment of the game. The hero's larger goal may be to save the princess, but he has many levels or missions to accomplish in between, such as slaying the dragon and finding the magic sword.

Shelley was also challenged by the idea of creating a philosophy of game design to help his team members understand the experience of being entertained by playing a computer game. "When we understand that," adds Shelley, "we can repeatedly create [successful] entertainment, not just hope we will."

As an industry veteran, Shelley was making and playing games even before he became involved with computers and console systems. "I was working for a board game company in Baltimore, Maryland, in the late 1980s, when a friend introduced me to a game called *Pirates!* on his Commodore 64."

After being extremely impressed with the game, Shelley happily discovered that the company was located in the same city where he lived. He immediately made the switch to computer games and applied for a job at Microprose, a company now owned by Atari. At the time, the company was producing some of the most innovative computer game titles, which included the submarine epic *Silent Service* as well as the aforementioned *Pirates!* Many of these games are now considered classics.

This didn't mean that Shelley immediately started to create his own games. In fact, because of his radical career change, he actually began at the bottom.

I took a lower salary to start, volunteered for some of the ugly jobs most people didn't want, and tried to be a good employee in every way. I tried to learn both good things to do and mistakes to avoid from my colleagues. The opportunity to work there made all the difference in my [later] career.

A Day in the Life of a Game Designer

Early on in the production cycle, the design team will get together in a small group and talk about ideas for the next game. They will create a design document that will detail exactly who the characters are, what obstacles they must overcome, and the plot of the story. Ultimately, the lead designer is in charge of producing and maintaining this document. "You have to be able to convey ideas in a form that the people both in and outside your team can understand," says Acclaim Entertainment's Berenger Fish. Throughout the project, the team will have to update the design document to avoid confusion when elements change.

Deadlines during the development cycle are often referred to as milestones. These milestones let the team members, especially the producers and designers, know how quickly or slowly progress is being made. The designer must carefully consider a game's quality on a daily basis. He or she must deliver the best results in the end, which is often more important than adhering to a constantly rigid schedule. Still, it is uncommon for games to be delayed because delays can often cost money, forcing the game's production over its intended budget.

A typical day of a level designer will differ greatly from a lead designer's. He or she might focus on designing a level and planning where the enemies attack. Or a level designer might concentrate on actually building an area of the world, by adding trees and buildings, in the event that art has not yet been created. In most cases, proxies are simply empty boxes that take up space in the world until the real art is dropped in later.

Although a level designer often begins his or her work independently, he or she later relies on other designers and art production members. When Acclaim Entertainment designer Berenger Fish started in the industry in the late 1990s, for instance, level designers were more intimately involved in the appearance of each level. Production artists made texture sets, which are the tiles of art that comprise the surfaces of any computer game's world. For example, if the design document called for a brick building, a graphic artist would make a tile of brick art that could be repeated throughout the building to create its surface. If the design document called for the appearance of an underground subway, the designer would ask the art department to create tiles of concrete floors and walls. After the tiles were finished, the level designers would build that underground level.

"The person who creates the look of the level [also] designs the game's [operation] of the level," Fish explains. "Now that games are more realistic in terms of graphics, these two disciplines are separated into the guy who can make the game [operate] and the guy who can make it look good."

But because designers don't always work together so closely, level designers often lay out games by using proxy geometry, that is, by creating predetermined sized shapes that "stand in" for the art until it is created later. At the same time, they will speak with the artists about what the game levels should look like. For example, in a construction yard, Fish says, "the designer might tell the artist that there's a fence here and you can put whatever you'd like behind that fence. So the designer defers to the artist for the look of the level."

A designer can realistically complete a proxy level without having the finished art or programming resources in it. Perhaps the programming department hasn't finished working on the enemy AI (the artificial intelligence that tells characters how to make decisions), or the art department is working on the buildings a designer needs (he or she will use proxies in the shapes of the proposed buildings instead). Once all the resources come in, the designer who worked on the proxy level may finish it, or if the lead designer believes that will take too long, several level designers will collaborate to complete the project. At some companies, Fish adds, one designer may work on one level only, changing it and fine-tuning it for more than a year and a half. In that case, a lead designer has to make sure that the quality between levels is consistent "so that a bunch of enemies don't stand around in one level but are jumping through windows to get the player in another level."

Alex Garden, CEO of Relic Entertainment, stresses that being a designer means being part of a nonstop process. When summarizing what he feels makes a game great, he says, "It is one that millions and millions of people want to play. I don't feel limited to a particular platform or genre. Trying to be the best in the world at more than one thing is a recipe for disaster."

As a result, Garden stresses that he is always coming up with the next game idea, yet he remains focused on designing the kinds of games for which his company is known. Sometimes this also means that he can't just concentrate on games that he'd want to play. "The industry has really matured," he admits, "but the stakes are very high and it isn't practical to be making personal passion products in triple-A titles."

Relic Entertainment, such as most game development studios, thinks constantly about making games that the majority of people will want to play. For Garden, this means having as many as three games at various stages of development at any given time. This constant design and development requires an ability to think clearly about several different games at once. Designers need to keep their plot lines, characters, and settings completely separate. Juggling simultaneous projects is a lot to handle for game designers, especially because most games are also produced for multiple platforms. This means that any particular game might come out for Microsoft's Xbox, Sony's PlayStation 2, Nintendo's GameCube, and PCs at the same time.

Designers have to remain on schedule, which requires a day-to-day balancing of all the important tasks while making sure that everyone is accomplishing his or her specific job. The lead designer assigns level designers to work on specific problems. Designers then meet with producers in order to update the progress on the game and explain what still needs to be accomplished. The design team also works on the script, unless the lead designer hires a dedicated writer.

A designer has to continually ask him- or herself questions about the game. What will make it stand out from its competitors' games? Is there enough action and excitement in the game so that its players won't become bored? What technologies are the programmers working on that could open up new play possibilities? *Sims* creator Will Wright stresses that "how you choose to answer all these questions will determine your success."

Computer game designers should be ready for the unexpected, since each day is likely to be different from the last, even when projects generally result in a regular flow of work. "There is a certain rhythm or cycle to it," explains Wright. "At the start of a project it will be very freeform as the team is building and early prototyping is under way."

Important deadlines, such as finishing a basic version of the game that contains just a bit of interaction that could be shown to the press at an industry trade

show such as E3, will require even more work by the designers—a situation that is often referred to as crunch time. Wright continues, "These peaks will build both in frequency and intensity up until the 'final crunch.' This is the hardest part of the job, getting the game out the door." Sometimes the licensor comes into the design studio to check on the process or approve a game's new feature. Other days, members of the press come by for a preview of a new game. Whatever the case, the design team's job is to ensure that the game is up and running and that it's being represented in a positive light.

CAREER GROWTH

Being a designer, especially a lead designer, means a lot of responsibilities, but it also offers the most creative control in the industry. You get to establish the ground rules for the team, and determine the schedule of when you and the rest of the team will work. But most important, you'll get to take your vision for a game and see it come true. And while this may sound like the top of the heap in terms of careers in the computer game world, there are still plenty of opportunities to do more.

Unless you plan on starting your own company, you'll probably be a lead designer for someone else's project. This can include making a new version of an existing game— often called a port—to a new platform. Additionally, you might be charged with creating an expansion pack or add-on (new missions, levels, and/or features) for an existing game, or possibly creating a sequel. While these can be exciting tasks, many designers would rather create original games based on their own unique ideas.

Even for those who have been able to make their own successful games, there are plenty of additional opportunities in the world of computer game design, including starting a company and trying to be even more innovative. As Garden and Shelley will attest, it is one thing

Tips from the Professionals

Brandon Fish, Producer, Acclaim Entertainment:

If you want to be a game designer, maybe you want to show your creative writing skills or even write your own game design without actually making the game. Show how the game would work and show that you can put those ideas on paper.

Sometimes a designer will come up through the QA department [because he or she has started at the company as a QA tester]. QA testers work hard at doing what they're supposed to do, which is to "break" the game [while searching it for programming errors]. [But] there's a difference between playing the game and designing the game. You need to understand that difference between what will be fun and what can be done and to repair what is broken. A designer can't just say, 'This isn't fun.' He needs to be able to explain why or how [the game] can be fixed.

The best thing is to do [get a job as a] QA [tester] during summers in between semesters so you can see what it is that goes into a game. You can see the evolution of a game as it goes from nothing to finished product. But when it comes to your résumé for design, it comes down to skill. You have to have a good portfolio of levels you've designed. You want to have a portfolio of both single-player and multiplayer levels because you don't know what the company might be working on. Include a sample of levels on a CD and send it along with your résumé.

to make games for someone else, but it is entirely more rewarding to make your own games at your own company.

The salary for a designer varies greatly, depending on his or her experience. Lead designers make substantially more than level designers. Salaries can range from $50,000 to $100,000 and up, with lead designers on the higher end of the salary scale.

CHAPTER 5

PRODUCERS

Whenever you watch a movie, listen to a CD, or play a computer game, the work that you see and hear was shaped, at least in part, by a producer. Films, sound recordings, and computer games all have producers. But what does the producer actually produce?

A producer is responsible for getting the project—film, album, and even computer game—through every stage of the creation cycle. He or she brings people on board to work on the project, sets a budget, and maintains deadlines. The producer is the guiding force from start to finish. In short, the question is not, "What does the producer do?" but "What *doesn't* the producer do?"

The producer's ultimate task is to keep everyone on the same page. In this role, you'll hold a lot of meetings between departments. These discussions will include designers to ensure that they have all the necessary information, as well as with the art department to see that all the art elements for the game are in place, with programmers to determine that bugs are being eliminated, and with lead testers to learn if there are new bugs. Finally, other meetings will include the entire department so that everyone working on the game can communicate about changes. The publisher might also be present during these group meetings, and he or she will request periodic updates on the status of the game's design as it progresses.

Because the cost of making a computer game can run into millions, a producer must be careful with his or her budget. He or she must consult with the designers to make certain that the project is doable within the restraints of both the budget and the deadline. The deadline is especially important. Most games are ideally sold in the autumn, around holiday season. But this also means that a game must be finished months beforehand so that it may be approved by the publisher and console makers, and so that hundreds of thousands (sometimes millions) of copies can be made and shipped to stores across the country and even the world.

Again, as in the case of this and all other jobs in the industry, communication skills are crucial. No one wants to spend needless amounts of time listening to progress updates that are outdated or unnecessary. A producer needs to be aware of all aspects of a given job at all times. He or she also has to be able to answer the questions of any department's team leader, those of the president of the company, and everyone in between. The producer is also responsible for the morale of his or her creative team. Supplying a take-out dinner for everyone during a particularly stressful day is commonplace. A talented and accomplished producer is a jack-of-all-trades who is ready and willing to pitch in wherever he or she might be needed.

Whenever a computer game is based on an existing intellectual property, such as the NFL or a popular movie, the producer must add another layer of communication to the mix. The company that owns the intellectual property is called the licensor, and it must approve everything that is in the proposed game: the look of the characters, all the lyrics in the music, and all the text.

Brandon Fish, a producer at Acclaim Studios, has worked with the NBA on games such as *NBA Jam* and *NBA Inside Drive*. "They're very, very strict about how logos look and what you can [and can't] do in the game. We had an outdoor court on the beach and some of the girls in the crowd were wearing bikinis. They said, 'That's fine, just don't make the girls too sexy.' We couldn't do a Vegas court because they didn't want slot machines in the background. It's their intellectual property and they want to make sure it's used how they want it to be used." In many ways, working on an unlicensed project can be more creative because the production team only has to answer to the publisher and the console manufacturers.

REINING IN THE TEAM

The producer has to handle tough decisions. Because everyone on the development team is generally passionate about the game he or she is working on, it isn't unusual to keep adding more and more features to the game as it progresses. At a certain point, however, a producer must step in and help maintain the game's focus. Deadlines are made for a reason, and sometimes an extra feature must be cut—no matter how cool it would be to include it—in order to finish on schedule.

Even though a computer game producer is a high-ranking job in the industry, don't be surprised to find these men and women burning the midnight oil since this position is rarely a nine-to-five job. According to Fish,

Although I could go home at 5 PM, part of my responsibility is to make sure the team has good morale. If I go home before everybody else, it's not going to make everybody feel good. This [tight] schedule [usually] comes from poor planning at the beginning, [as well as] changing resources. The amount of people you have changes, the needs always change. There's never been a project I've worked on that didn't need something major added in the middle of it. Or sometimes the game just isn't fun, so we have to fix it. Long hours are almost expected. When a game is trying to get out the door, that's the way it's going to be. It's almost required.

An assistant or associate producer takes direction from the producer, manages a particular aspect of the game, take notes at meetings, and basically assists the producer in whatever way possible. He or she is essentially a producer-to-be and will typically rise from the ranks of the game testers. Working as an assistant or associate producer is a great position in which to learn all the ins and outs of the production cycle.

The design document outlines the project: the story (how the plot progresses and twists), the quests (or missions that the player must carry out), the system design (the nuts and bolts of the game), and the interface (how a player controls his character and player information on the screen).

"We also detail out as many of the side quests as [early as] possible," explains Leonard Boyarsky, joint CEO/producer of Troika Games. "The quests are the most malleable part of this whole document because they change in relation to the capabilities of the engine we're using. We refine them once they are implemented to make sure they are fun to play." Side quests (missions not related to the main story that can often be fun and challenging diversions) are often added as the game's development cycle continues. The game's main story may also undergo changes and revisions depending on its pacing. For example, if a part of the game is slow and boring, the producer, in tandem with the design team, may decide to add a plot twist to spice up the action.

The interface also evolves during production. "Try to get it working early in your game's development cycle so that it can be tweaked to get the feel right over the course of the entire process," Boyarsky advises. The way in which a player interacts with a game is crucial. It has to be simple enough to learn quickly but complex enough to do a number of intricate moves. No matter how good the game's story may be; it won't mean anything to a player frustrated by an unintuitive interface.

As you might imagine, some games are more complicated to produce than others. Role-playing games tend to be very complicated, with a multitude of branching plots and a huge inventory of assets (characters, creatures, and environments). "The amount of testing has to be very [detailed] because there are so many places to go and things to do," says Acclaim's Brandon Fish. On the flip side, puzzle games tend to be more straightforward, although you might have less time to work on them.

A slightly more obscure role on the production team is that of the localization producer. Generally, he or she will oversee several games at once with one translator and one writer per game. The localization producer's job is to take the text and dialogue of, for example, a Japanese game and translate it into English, or "localize" it. The editorial team will also write marketing information and communicate with the company's public relations department. Sometimes entire elements of a game must be changed. In certain Japanese games, for example, players pick up rice balls to recover health. "In most parts of the United States," says Bill Trinen, associate localization producer for Nintendo, "they don't know what rice balls are: they'll see a white ball wrapped in seaweed. We'll have the art department change that to a sandwich or hamburger."

Between all the cultural differences between any two countries in the world, some changes can be quite drastic. For *Animal Crossing*, Trinen and his team added a Thanksgiving-like harvest festival, something the Japanese do not celebrate. The localization producer chose to have a turkey character appear on the fourth Thursday of every November. The turkey received a letter from the mayor, that was written in such a way that the turkey was never sure whether he was being invited to eat dinner or to be eaten for dinner. To solve this problem, he spent all day hiding in shadows. Players of *Animal Crossing* searched for him. If they located him, he'd give them a television with a football image on the screen. Trinen's team worked with the development team in Japan to execute the idea, which only appeared in the U.S. version of the game.

QUALIFICATIONS

A computer game producer must also be extremely responsible, communicative, and organized since everyone working on the game's development will defer to him or her for advice. A producer must be familiar enough with all aspects of the game's development so that he or she can offer that advice quickly or make a wide range of decisions. He or she has to know what everyone is working on and how his or her individual progress relates to the overall condition of the project.

In addition to having excellent organizational skills, a producer must know how to set and maintain deadlines and budgets, run productive meetings, and communicate with a variety of people who have different needs. A producer never says, "I don't know." Familiarity with every facet of how a game gets made is crucial. How else would he or she know how to predict and track the game's development?

Leadership, time management, and organization are all necessary attributes of the person in the producer role. These skills are most effective when married to hands-on practical knowledge of the everyday environment of game development. This means that the producers who are most effective were, at one time or another, QA testers, level designers, production assistants, or have worked their way through the ranks of one of the various departments (art, programming, design). Working as a production assistant is perhaps the best possible way in which to get closer to the producer's position, however, because it offers a chance to be exposed to the entire creative process.

A producer's duties will vary, depending on the size of a company. For instance, Leonard Boyarsky, joint CEO of Troika Games, once acted as producer on top of his normal creative design position of drawing concept art, texturing characters, and even writing dialogue. Since Troika recently doubled in size, it now has the need for a distinct management team. "As you grow, the need for individuals to concentrate on one job or aspect of the game becomes much greater," he says. For a producer who has risen through the ranks from an art department or design team, he must make a trade-off between the business side and the creative side. Boyarsky spends his days executing contracts, working with publishers, and getting the press interested in the game instead of working in a creative capacity, which he prefers. "These are all things that take me away from working on the game itself, which is why we all got into this industry in the first place," he adds. "I don't know anyone who got into this industry for the thrill of negotiating a contract."

A localization producer must focus on writing and language skills. Nintendo's Bill Trinen had been studying Japanese for ten years and had lived in Japan for three before landing his first job in the industry. "It's more than merely studying the language," he says. "You must master it. Learn history and culture," he adds. "You might have Japanese text or dialogue referring to an aspect of Japanese culture or a folk story. Identify the point of reference and find a parallel event in American or Western history."

Another important aspect of being an effective producer is the ability to manage time. Producers must be able to consider a span of time, understand how quickly or slowly a project is developing, and make decisions based on that information. According to Boyarsky, time management is a key component to the success or failure of any game in development. He says, "Personally, I prefer to make a tight, detailed schedule for the first few months of production, and then get more general [later]. Unfortunately, [most] publishers don't generally [manage time in that way] and they want a strict, detailed schedule for the whole project before you've even started. This is troublesome, because it is difficult to see exactly what new challenges will [appear] down the road that you can't possibly predict. It is much easier to schedule a [game's] sequel, or one where you are [already] familiar with the technology."

A DAY IN THE LIFE OF A PRODUCER

Typically, a producer will spend his or her day in meetings. For example, he or she might have a meeting with the management of the studio to give them an update on how the project is going. Later, a producer might call the publisher to give its president an update. The producer needs to stay ahead of whatever the publisher's needs may be at every moment. Are new screen shots needed for a promotional event because the game's look has changed? Has the game's entire vision or mission changed during its development? As mentioned before, a producer has to remain on top of his or her art and programming staff to determine what everyone is doing. A producer will also meet with teams on an individual basis to see that their needs are met.

As the deadline approaches, when employees are working during crunch time, a producer's duties become a little different. "You're spending all your time going through the bug database, making sure that testers have gone through all areas of the game, making sure the bugs get fixed, or spitting the bug back to the testers for more information before we can fix it," says Acclaim's producer Brandon Fish. "Then you do that twenty-four hours a day until the game is done."

Creating schedules and holding people to them are a huge part of the life of a computer game producer. Those are his or her primary duties. Falling behind does not only mean that the game will be late, it could miss an important release date, which could result in poor sales. Fish continues, "The schedule changes all the time. There are always things that somebody needs to get into the game, whether that's a licensor who requires its logo to be somewhere, or a feature gets cut or added because the competition's got something that we need to match or [beat]."

Because the responsibility of meeting deadlines ultimately falls to the producer, he or she must act as a taskmaster of sorts. "Nobody likes the producer," Fish says. "You've got milestones to show the publisher that you have what you said you'd have on that date. Sometimes there's negotiation: 'Well, we didn't quite meet this, but we're well ahead in this other area.' Ultimately it's up to the publisher whether or not the milestone was reached. Some third-party developers don't get paid unless a milestone is met. That puts a lot of pressure on everybody."

According to Leonard Boyarksy, joint CEO of Troika Games, being a producer is almost totally about making sure deadlines are met, though there is also pressure to make sure the game is as good as it can be. This is a difficult balance, but the producer is there to make that balance work. Boyarsky begins with a rigid schedule at the outset and then loosens it up as the project progresses. "You can never predict what may come up down the road," he says.

Being a computer game producer is also about multitasking, as Boyarsky explains:

Even when a producer's only responsibility is management and "producing," I'd still say they wear different hats to a certain degree. For one thing, they have to interact with all the different leads and understand what they are doing; whether it is art, design, or programming. And during the crunch, near the end of a project, it's not unlikely that producers [will] find themselves testing the game as well as lending a hand wherever they can to ensure the game gets done.

CAREER GROWTH

You're not going to become a producer right out of college, so your first step is to learn what it takes to take a project to completion. A lot of producers get their starts as QA testers. Once they've shown an aptitude for the business, they might be offered jobs as assistant producers if these positions become available. Other times, a lead or assistant lead in one of the departments might move over to a production role.

Twenty or so years ago, people would write entire programs in BASIC (a simple programming language) and get them published in magazines to get their names around. That has changed a lot. Today, there are entire schools such as DigiPen and Full Sail (refer to the For More Information section at the back of this book for more details) that are dedicated to getting people into the industry. "If you can get through [those schools], then you pretty much have a job anywhere," Brandon Fish explains.

But it helps to have a clear focus. "When people are hiring, especially some of the smaller studios, you have to have a desire to play games. People in this industry who aren't [true] gamers or [who] don't enjoy playing games don't last very long," he continues. "There are a lot of hours that go into a game, and if you're not passionate about what you're doing, it shows." For those who do have a passion for gaming, the gig pays $30,000 to $50,000 for a position as an assistant producer, and past the $80,000 mark for an experienced producer.

CHAPTER 6

PROGRAMMERS

A programmer literally builds a game from the ground up. He or she writes the code (the lines written on a computer in a programming language) that forms the practical aspects of the project. Programming is accomplished by a team of people who work together to bring the designers' vision to reality.

Typically, a team breaks down into several types of specialized programmers. An engine programmer, for instance, develops a game's foundation, or its engine, on which the rest of the game will be built. An engine or tools programmer will create the scripting tools and level editors that the designers will use to bring their design to life. (A level editor is a software tool that allows the designer, or in some cases even players, to design unique maps or levels to the game). Fashioning such tools is no small task. The better the tools and the easier the user interface (the way in which the designer interacts with the program) the faster the game progresses.

Communication between members of the programming team is obviously necessary, but when it comes to a dialogue between the lead programmer, producer, and lead designer, it is imperative. Both producers and designers must be able to implement the plans in the design document. Failure to communicate properly can be one of the biggest obstacles for any programmer, and this can often lead to problems.

Perhaps the designers' wish list is impossible given the current technology, or the idea is too ambitious and the engine programmer will have to invent new coding solutions from scratch. In other cases, the designers' intentions may not be ambitious enough. Once the designers see the capabilities of the game's architecture (built by the programmers), they will begin to push the boundaries of the original design. This is only possible when all the team leaders talk to each other and understand the design department's goals.

CS 120 High-Level Programming I – The C Programming Language (3 Cr.)
Prerequisites: None
Concurrent Course: CS 100
Description: The objective of this course is to present the concepts of high-level programming. The C++ programming language is the language of choice. The course starts with a short presentation of what constitutes a programming language. Presentation of C++ follows. Then the course covers lexical and grammatical elements of C++. Finally, the course focuses on the presentation of object-oriented paradigms.

CS 170 High-Level Programming II – The C++ Programming Language (3 Cr.)
Prerequisite: CS 120
Description: This course is a continuation of CS 120, High-Level Programming I. This course starts where the previous left off, with the study of object-oriented programming. OOP is discussed in detail and will be used throughout the course. Students will be introduced to more advanced concepts of higher-level programming using the C++ programming language.

CS 180 Operating System I, Man-Machine Interface (3 Cr.)
Prerequisites: CS 100, CS 120
Description: This course presents the various components of the memory map of a computer and the techniques involved in writing software based on operating system calls.

This excerpt from the DigiPen Institute of Technology catalog features several examples of classes taken by students at the college level who are working toward a degree in computer programming. Besides being known as a top-notch school for people seeking a career in the computer gaming industry, DigiPen is well known for its aggressive job-placement service for graduates.

"Communication problems range from someone getting angry when you disagree with them, to telling two people the same thing and each of them understanding something differently," explains Zied Rieke, lead designer and programmer at Infinity Ward. No matter what the reason for a breakdown in communication, it must be resolved. "When you have thirty people who are all supposed to be working toward the same goal and all the interdependencies that go along with that, solid communication is an absolute must."

Beginning as a programmer can be as simple as toying with built-in tools supplied for just that purpose. Sometimes the developer will include a version of the level editor with the game. In Activision's *Tony Hawk* games, for example, players can lay out their own skate park, which they can then use to play the game. These features are a great opportunity for aspiring game makers to hone their skills, as discussed in Chapter 2.

The engine is the foundation. If it is a three-dimensional (3-D) world, the programmers might concentrate on creating a virtual space within which characters can move freely, light casts realistic shadows, water flows and reflects other objects, and where fire doesn't just burn, it shoots sparks into the air. But someone still needs to tell the computer characters how to act and react when the player invades this space. Creating this artificial intelligence (AI) is the job of the AI programmer.

The goal of the AI programmer is to write rules of behavior for the computer characters, which, when followed, generate intelligent actions based on interpretations of any given situation. That means if your player character charges into a room with guns blazing, the three computer characters should react accordingly. Suppose one is near a desk: he should move behind the desk for cover. If another is caught in the open, he should not stand still but move out of the way and return fire. If the third is behind the door and you haven't seen him yet, he should wait until you are farther inside the room so he can attack you from behind. That's smart AI, and it all has to happen instantly in real time. Good programmers find their work in this area coinciding with work in robotics and psychology.

Recently, AI got even more complicated. According to David Perry of Shiny Entertainment, the newest computer games are expected to have more complicated responses, which mean more complex programming:

> *The recent hurdle for computer game programmers [was] "Applied Physics," meaning you can knock stuff around everywhere in game worlds and people can collapse into rag-dolls. That's old news now, so people are starting to look into [more] advanced AI where characters can understand and even form sentences themselves . . . The goal is to make characters with real personalities that can react interestingly to complex situations.*

But programmers aren't expected to know everything from standard military procedure to the decision process of an NFL middle linebacker. Often, a freelance consultant is brought in to explain the ins and outs of his or her profession to the designers and programmers. For example, Captain Dale Dye, a Vietnam veteran and consultant on such films as *Saving Private Ryan* and *Platoon*, lent his expertise to Electronic Arts' *Medal of Honor* series. John Madden, a former Oakland Raiders coach and current television analyst, lends not only his name, but also his years of NFL experience to EA Sports' *Madden* football series.

Although we may speak of 3-D games and worlds, these things still take place on a flat, two-dimensional (2-D) screen. The job of a graphics or special effects programmer is to translate 3-D objects and effects into 2-D space.

With the rise in the number of multiplayer games, some projects will call for a networking programmer who specializes in making sure the multiplayer experience

Careers in the Computer Game Industry

runs smoothly while taking into consideration such issues as security, billing (some games charge money to play online), synchronization, and Internet protocols.

Whether the game is intended for a console, PC, or handheld platform, there are limits dictated by the processing speed of each platform. Occasionally, compromises have to be made. Every feature, whether it's the fire effects in the game engine or the military tactics in the AI, uses processing speed. Hard choices might have to be made if that limit is exceeded. Again, communication plays a big part. A common challenge for programmers is making a feature appear to do what you want it to do without using up much processing power. That might mean scaling the feature back a little bit (or even a lot). That sounds disappointing, but remember, the processing power of platforms is always increasing. What is impossible today may be par for the course tomorrow. Still, this is one of the most difficult problems faced by today's computer programmers.

According to Zied Rieke, lead designer and programmer at Infinity Ward:

The most difficult hurdle I face is trying to figure out what features the game really needs versus what features [it] can do without. We never have a shortage of ideas of how our game or any other game could be improved. Name one shortcoming you see in a review of one of Infinity's games and I can bet we talked about it and had several possible solutions. But if you want to make games that ship when they are scheduled, you have to learn that you can't do everything. So I have the difficult and painful task of figuring out what is [most] important.

QUALIFICATIONS

While a solid education will give you a foundation for any position in the computer industry, it is especially important for programmers, who should pay particular attention to learning mathematics and programming languages. A computer science degree will help immensely. This is where you'll learn the fundamentals of computer programming.

Visual C + + is a common programming language in the industry. Good programmers will have experience with C (another programming language), calculus, data structures, 3-D mathematics, and algorithms (formulae for solving complicated math problems).

Other skills can benefit a prospective programmer, too, such as a working knowledge of the common software programs that produce graphics and animations such as Flash. Although you won't need to master any graphics or sound design programs, you should have an understanding of how they might affect the overall program.

Other useful skills, particularly for AI programmers, include knowledge of neural networks and fuzzy logic. These are concepts built on algorithms that determine how things work in the game. Every character in a game—and this includes any objects that actually move and react such as cars, monsters, and spaceships—has its own AI. This is essentially software code that works with the rest of the game and dictates how these characters or objects react. For example, in an adventure game, this type of code, which responds to how you react, could control the guards at the king's palace. As you move closer, the AI reacts accordingly. Do the guards recognize you as a friend, greeting you warmly or allowing you to pass? Or do they see you as an enemy, moving to intercept your passage?

Either decision can result in a complex series of events. Every action on the screen has some programmed code that determines what happens in the game. Although you can't walk through walls in the real world, in the game world, software code could allow this as a chosen function.

As an aspiring programmer, you don't need to be an expert in every facet of game programming. "Teams are big enough to handle specialists," Perry says. "For example, if applied physics is your gig, then all we expect you to be is an expert in that field."

A Day in the Life of a Programmer

As a programmer, you'll spend many hours in front of a computer. Most of this time will not be spent looking at detailed graphics, but individual lines of software code. These lines of source code are the heart and soul of a computer game. The individual lines are written in a specific programming language. Every single line is as important as any other for the game to properly function.

When a game isn't functioning the way it should, it is because there is a mistake in one of these lines or because something doesn't add up correctly. These errors or bugs are often found by QA testers and itemized in written reports, which are then given to the programmer who responds by fixing this "broken" code.

The heart of a programmer's job is solving problems. "The first step is to understand the domain of the problem and what needs to be solved in terms of specific results," explains Clinton Keith, vice president and director of technology at Sammy Studios. "Then the problem is broken down into smaller parts, or requirements, until you get to the point where each requirement or sub-problem [can be] solved from the bottom up. One key thing to do is to keep sight of the big picture."

Programmers break tasks down in order to focus on smaller, simpler problems. What may originally appear very complex, such as a giant skyscraper, can be built using thousands of smaller building blocks, explains Perry of Shiny Entertainment. "When you watch a soccer game on screen, just know that a programmer had to think about every single part [of that game]: not just a bouncing ball and some players, but how to detect every surface of the field—the posts, the players, how the ball spins and bounces, every character against every other character,

[and] how a character can avoid another character."

As an analogy, Perry suggests a thought experiment. If you were asked to get an egg from the fridge, how many steps could you break that down into? "If you said 'go to fridge, open door, take egg,' that's a start, but if you said, 'send impulse from brain to leg muscle to move leg forward,' then you would be [thinking like] a programmer," Perry says.

While meetings between members crop up from time to time, the details of the daily work schedule are filled with hours in front of the computer screen. "Ideally a programmer will code as much as possible," Keith emphasizes, adding that a lot of the aforementioned ability to problem- solve figures into the agenda. This is where he or she steps in and tries to fix these problems so his or her programmers can get down to business. "I

An Example of C++

In order to help illustrate what a typical computer language looks like, here is the message "Hello World" in a C + + program:

//Purpose: To show the rules of
C + + programming
This is the **comment line**. It is included to communicate with other programmers, usually to tell him or her what purpose the program will serve. It always starts with two slashes.

include < iostream.h >
The second line in a program is called a **directive**. It tells the compiler, or processor of the program, what he or she should be looking for. In this case, the compiler should search for a file.

int main ( )
This line is called a **function header**. It introduces the main function of the program and tells the computer to begin.

{cout < < "Hello, World!\n";
This line, called an **expression** statement, is the first command that the computer will obey.

return 0;
This is called the **return statement**, also ending in a semicolon.

} // main
The end of the program.

have to spend most of my time trying to eliminate as much of the overhead [as I can] from the programmers."

This so-called overhead is the result of a breakdown in communication. Keith describes hours when he has to get away from his desk and spend time with individual programmers in one-on-one situations so small problems can be identified early. But he stresses, "programmers like solving 'real' problems, not problems that are caused by human organization factors!"

Having a team member such as Keith in place lets Sammy Studios keep the programming teams productive. "I spend a lot of my time dealing with cross-disciplinary issues that come up between technology and art, design, marketing, and management."

Finding the answers isn't always easy. Rieke, programmer at Infinity Ward, admits that a lot of programming involves trial and error. "Often there is no way of knowing the right answers without trying a bunch of stuff until you find out what works."

CAREER GROWTH

Programmers need to be highly skilled. They must remain current with the latest developments with regard to both software and hardware. Computer games continually get more complicated. Because of these demands, a good programmer will strive to keep on top of new technology.

Although programmers work as a team, beginner programmers will often assist more experienced members, helping to fix existing code. The starting salary for a beginning programmer is between $40,000 and $80,000. Experienced programmers can often fetch as much as $120,000.

You can expect to start programming under the direction of more experienced programmers while working on someone else's engine. As your skills increase, you'll advance to the design aspect of programming to create your own worlds, or even have the chance to develop a new engine that becomes the basis of a new game. Whether seasoned or inexperienced, being a computer programmer is a rewarding job for those people who don't mind working with line after line of source code and who are not put off by searching for the theoretical needle in a haystack.

Tips from the Professionals

Zied Rieke, Lead Designer, Programmer, Infinity Ward
We all play games in our spare time and recommend games to each other. Personally, I play as many games as I can, looking for some new bit of game play or some cool new advance in interfaces or graphics techniques. I'm never afraid to consider something I saw in another game.

Clinton Keith, Vice President and Technology Director, Sammy Studios
There's been quite a bit of literature published over the last few years about practices such as Agile Iteration, XP, and Scrum, [some of the latest software programs that designers are using]. As teams get larger, the overhead of having everyone work together with any large degree of effectiveness becomes more challenging.

David Perry, President, Founder, Shiny Entertainment
Study hard and practice in any spare time you have. [Programming] is a very competitive field. [Competitors] are literally sleeping under their desks so that they can get ahead of the other teams. Know that it's a massive mental challenge. It is, however, very rewarding, both financially and in the relationships among gamers and the game-making community.

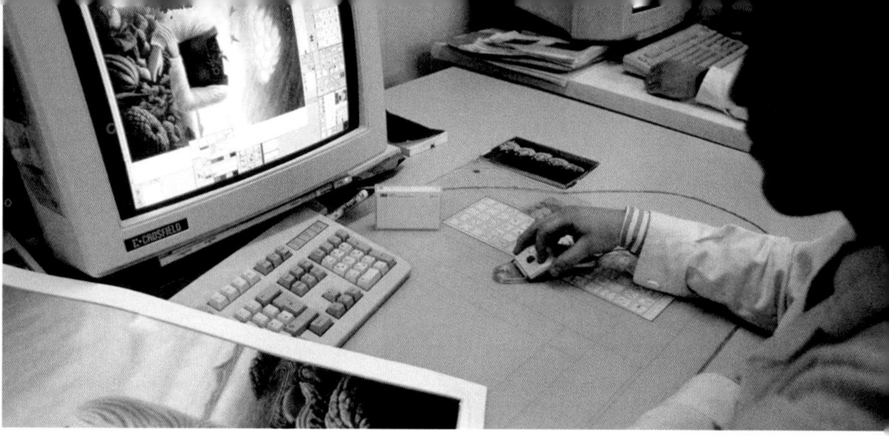

CHAPTER 7

GRAPHIC ARTISTS AND ANIMATORS

Artists and animators make the images that eventually appear on your television set or computer monitor. They bring these images to life with complex and lifelike movements. Artists create the entire visual look of the game, from the shape of each character's nose to the bricks of a castle wall.

With initial direction from the design document created by the producer and designers, artists will begin by creating concept sketches on paper. These are initial sketches for the different characters in the game as well as the environments in which they will live. This task is usually followed by a session where other members of the design team will offer their feedback during a presentation of concepts, though this introduction process can vary.

While animators design how a game's characters and other elements move, the art team focuses on specific visual details. Artists design textures (the surfaces of all the objects in a game), tiles (pieces of a game's environment that repeat), backdrops, and skins (the outside appearance of a character or vehicle—the model itself is handled by the animators). Tiles are often created to save time. If the game calls for a snowy scene, for example, one section of snow can be created and then repeated in a tile format as needed.

If the art team is large enough, it may contain artists who only draw concept sketches and others who only design textures. The more skills you have as a designer, the more valuable you are to any art team.

The art director (also known as the creative director) leads the entire art department. As a team leader, you should understand every aspect of creating digital art, as well as being able to render your ideas on paper if needed. Art directors work closely with producers to

This early sketch helped set the tone of the Activision game *Call of Duty* and provided a guideline to the graphic designers. Surprisingly enough, much of the early art for computer games is done the old-fashioned way, on paper, and then revised and edited in advanced software programs such as Adobe Photoshop and Illustrator.

identify problems and maintain deadlines. The animation director has the same duties with his or her animation team. At this level, an animation director more often has the responsibility of attending meetings and managing those artists under him or her than actually creating animation.

According to Corey Dangel, art director at Microsoft's Games Studio, a typical day for an art director is anything but typical:

> *Every day is unique and challenging. I meet with a lot of people from a variety of disciplines. I try to coordinate the work going on in all of the different teams, from conceptual work to modeling, from texturing to animating, environments to special effects. It's a complicated machine with a lot of moving parts. I try to keep the parts moving as freely as possible. One minute I'm talking to a concept artist about a new idea, the next I'm working with the computer programmers to make sure we're getting the most out of our graphics, then I might do a model review with the creature team. [All of this might be] followed by a meeting with the marketing group about what to feature in the next magazine article.*
>
> *Occasionally I get to work on a model or a texture, but that always takes a backseat to making sure the whole team is running as smoothly as possible. It's a fast-paced and very demanding job. And I love it.*

QUALIFICATIONS

In addition to a game's plot, character development, and method of play, the first things that reviewers and players notice are the quality and detail of its graphics. In order for the game to be thrilling, many players require that it also appear realistically. If the game's objective is to run racing cars around a muddy track, then the cars and players need to get dirty. If a player is rushing past his teammates toward the goal, then he or she should appear to be sweaty and stressed. The look of the game is tantamount to its eventual success or failure.

Many a great game was missed by the masses because it appeared dated. It is the job of the art team to make sure that a game looks as realistic as it possibly can, while also being innovative. And because of ever-changing system specifications and technology, including new 3-D graphics cards and new hardware on PC and console systems, artists and animators must constantly raise the bar with each new release.

Graphic artists and animators need to keep up on the latest technology, learn what it can do, and then take advantage of what it has to offer. They need to have a keen sense of color, an eye for detail, and even a sense of timing.

In this *Call of Duty* concept sketch, the artist was able to take information he learned about the game's proposed setting, a city invaded during World War II, and use those facts to create a realistic background. Hours and hours of planning and development go into the creation of any computer game, even before the actual animation and programming take place.

"I find that people with musical backgrounds, dancers, and actors tend to make very strong animators," explains Dangel, art director at Microsoft. "Of course good artistic skills are needed, but a lot of the best animators I know have spent a good amount of time learning how to act with their own bodies. It helps their work tremendously." Dangel adds that today's art schools include courses in animation, and he tells how his team at Microsoft relies on material found in Ollie Johnston and Frank Thomas's work, *The Illusion of Life*. Animation, as with music, has to do with timing and understanding rhythm and cadence. This can aid an animator in re-creating realistic movement of characters and creatures on screen.

The actual creation process for games combines elements of moviemaking with digital rendering via a

The artist's sketch lines can still be seen on this concept drawing, again for the Activision *Call of Duty* series. This is an example of concept art that will serve as a basis for a 3-D model of a tank in the game.

computer. Still, most animation teams use 2-D storyboards, and this process of rendering on paper remains invaluable. Storyboards feature the activity in a proposed animation, usually hand-rendered on paper or sometimes designed electronically, where a very rough scene is drawn out frame-by-frame. It resembles a comic strip and helps give the animators a sense of where characters and other objects will be placed and how they will move.

While animators draw storyboards, artists will be hard at work on the concept art, which is essentially sketches that represent what the game's designers and producers might have in mind. These might begin as simple pencil drawings and will eventually be re-created on a computer using a variety of programs including Alias Maya, Discreet 3DS Max, Avid Softimage, Adobe Illustrator, Corel Painter, and Adobe Photoshop. These characters begin to take on a 3-D format with the help of 3-D rendering software such as 3D Studio Max. But it takes more than software to create something unique.

"Every artist should have some training in fundamental art skills in the areas of illustration, fine arts, industrial design, graphic design, architecture, film, and photography," explains Emmanuel Valdez, Sammy Studios' vice president and creative director. He suggests that most schools' design courses will teach you to use those programs listed above to take the vision from paper to the screen.

Objects usually begin as simple wire frames, meaning that the object or character will begin as a visual image of small triangles that are attached. These triangles resemble a skeleton made of short pieces of wire. They are the visual basis of most 3-D computer game art. Naturally, you don't see the wires because other layers are placed on top of them. These layers, which can include skin and clothing, are called textures. All of these wire frames and textures are blended together to create what you see on the screen.

It is a complex process and requires experience with a lot of different software.

In fact, it takes many different software programs to create computer games. They are made up of lots of individually created objects that are then positioned together on the screen. "World and environment art is created in two places," explains Dangel. "Buildings and objects are modeled in Maya and textured using Adobe Photoshop. The landscape is generated in a proprietary tool custom-built for this game engine. It uses height fields to generate terrain, and it is very complicated."

In addition to the process of creating the backgrounds that make up the world, another specialized graphic artist needs to create the actual animations that give objects the ability to move. Whether these movements are from a character, a vehicle such as a plane or car, or even an exploding box, the objects need to be created separately from the rest of the art. But not all characters are animated in the same way and with the same methods.

According to Microsoft's Dangel, "Animation complexity depends a lot upon how prominent a character is in a game. The stars of the show, that is, the lead characters and epic bosses, get the most animation time. Characters that are seen frequently also receive extra attention. Their skeletons tend to be more complex to support the extra motion."

"Animation is a very exclusive and defined discipline," adds Valdez, who explains that animators typically have a background in traditional animation for film and computer. This might include learning to make simple flip-books (a book of many sequential drawings that when bound together and "flipped" by hand create a "moving" animation) or basic cartoon drawings, but the process does require specific training. "There are some excellent schools that specialize in animation. Cal Arts [in Valencia, California], is one of the best animation schools that offers courses in both traditional and computer animation. Many companies will hire animators with traditional animation experience and train them to use computer animation applications."

For fast-paced shooting and sports games, more and more the shift is toward a new technology aiding in the animation process called motion capture. This is a method of recording the motion and movement of objects and converting this as data into a 3-D space for a game. There are several ways that motion capture is done, but it often involves setting up several high-speed cameras and then transferring the film or computer footage into a computer. Motion capture is successful because individual areas of the subject are mapped in the computer so that its movement can be used with a character on a screen. This is usually done by having the subject wear a tightly fitted, solid color suit, along with smaller spheres of a different color such as tennis balls attached to arms, legs, and torso. Once in the computer, the image of the subject is overlaid on a similar color background as his or her suit so that he or she "disappears," but the tennis balls remain visible. The wire frames of a character can then be built around these tennis balls. When they move, so does the new character. The result is that a computer game character can move just as naturally as any person does in real life. Dangel, art director at Microsoft, says:

Motion capture is a powerful tool, but it's not right for every game. There's a lot to be said for beautifully crafted hand [drawn] animation. But motion capture enables us to catch the subtle nuances of a performance that might take animators far too long to create by hand. I'm not sure if motion capture is changing the way games are being played, but there is a tension between fluid motion and split-second reaction time. Game players seem to crave immediate control of their characters. Getting all those nuances from motion capture to play out, but still allowing a player to turn on a dime, poses some interesting challenges for [today's] game developers.

Many games still use traditional animation that is similar to cartoons, where each frame is individually rendered. Currently, both styles of creating movement in a game remain in place and will most likely coexist side-by-side for many years.

Animation applicants should create a portfolio (a sampling of their best work) on CD to include with their résumé. For a graphic artist, this should comprise a variety of 2-D and 3-D images, including people, buildings, and natural environments. An animator's portfolio, whether a short animated film or a computer-generated video, should demonstrate his or her ability to animate the motions of both people and objects, such as cars or wind-swept trees.

A DAY IN THE LIFE OF A GRAPHIC DESIGNER

"A typical computer game artist's day will comprise a mixed bag of artistic and technical challenges," states Sammy Studios' Emmanuel Valdez. "Modelers work in 3-D," he explains, "creating characters and environments based on concept art, while texture artists gather reference art from digital photographs and scans from books to use on environments and characters. Animators will spend their days using motion capture to create realistic, life-like movements for characters, and technical artists work with programmers to address issues such as how to get all the visual content into a game's console system."

An art director oversees this entire process, ensuring that the artists are delivering a consistent look and quality to the game's visual content. Valdez explains that achieving a solid visual look requires many individuals working well as a team. At smaller companies, there might be fewer artists to accomplish the same workload, perhaps as few as one or two. "These are just a sample of some of the different activities that happen in an average day in a game development company," Valdez continues.

As with every other aspect of a game's development, its visual look requires a lot of inspiration. Although a game's lead designer or producer may explain what he or she expects in any game, it is up to a team of artists to turn this expectation into a visual concept. Artists need to take the concept from the initial idea to a working model, and finally to the final design that is seen on the screen. This includes the characters, the world of the game, and every other element that the players experience. Finding this inspiration isn't always easy, but it is crucial to a game's success.

In order for a computer game to look realistic, plenty of research goes into the development of its overall appearance. In these preliminary sketches for *Call of Duty*, a team of visual artists experiments with a variety of period architectural elements in order to capture the look of a European city during World War II.

Tips from the Professionals

Corey Dangel, Art Director, Microsoft Games Studio
Learn how bodies move. Watch dancers and athletes. Learn how to act with your own body. Read The Illusion of Life *by Ollie Johnston and Frank Thomas.*

Emmanuel Valdez, Vice President and Creative Director, Sammy Studios
No matter what your specialty, you should have a basic background in fine arts, illustration, industrial design, architecture, and photography. Most schools will teach you the computer programs you'll need to know.

Joby Otero, Graphic Artist, Luxoflux
Nothing, I mean nothing, is as important as a good portfolio. Academic credentials can help, but they won't get you hired if you can't produce anything impressive with what you've learned.

Work at your skills every spare minute. As Salvador Dali said, "painter, paint!" This applies to 3-D artists every bit as much, if not more, than traditional painters. I find that I get rusty on the technical skills far faster than I do with sketching [and] painting. You must work that magic every day. Don't get caught up in the idea of creative block. That's just an excuse for laziness.

Don't be afraid to take a job that isn't exactly what you're looking for. You may not get to work on the kind of project you want right away, but industry experience counts for a lot in this business. You're a far less risky hire if you've shipped a title.

[If you've collaborated with someone on a project and you are using that for your demo reel to show to potential employers] include text explaining what percentage of what aspects of the work shown are yours. For example, modeling 50 percent, texturing 100 percent, etc. Include a printed document that covers this in more detail, for example, "I modeled the three-horned creature in the swimming pool and did all the texturing for all the creatures."

Brandon Fish, Producer, Acclaim Entertainment
If you're an artist, you have your own portfolio of 2-D or 3-D art or animation. You want to make sure you have an up-to-date portfolio. If you're in school for art, you'll be trained on how to put together your portfolio. If you're a programmer, sign on to a mod [a user-created modification of an existing game]. Make sure you finish school. If you don't finish school, it doesn't show that you've had the right amount of training.

"Inspiration can come from many sources, depending on the game's design, concepts, and genre," says Valdez. Designers look to movies, the works of other artists, other computer games, comic books, [or] even music. "Game design documents with descriptions of play, story concepts, and character ideas can inspire artists. [This] is one of the many reasons why game development is such an exciting and challenging job for artists."

Throughout the day, various members of the art team conduct research to make sure that new graphics look appropriate to the time and setting of the existing game. For example, war games often need to reflect the visual details of a specific time. Consistency is crucial, so art teams often build and refer to style boards showing how the existing art styles in any game compare. These can be simple printouts of the game's approved art elements, which are then collected. Style boards provide graphic samples to various departments so different team members can spot and identify visual trends in a game.

Dangel explains that he might occasionally hire concept artists to paint specific pieces to represent the mood of a game, or on other days, he'll rip pages from books, magazines, and catalogs to inspire the art team. These items are often placed on what is called a mood board, which might contain everything from sketches and doodles to complex paintings. The information from the mood board is then incorporated into the design document managed by the lead designer.

As the game begins to develop a visual identity, the animators take onscreen objects and give them realistic motion. For this process, animators often leave the office and take their inspiration from outside sources, such as the local zoo. Whether trying to replicate an animal's movement or even animating fantastic creatures, observing the movement of live animals can be especially helpful. At the zoo, animators can watch and track how similar real-life animals move. Film and television documentaries can help aid in the process by showing how bones, flesh, and muscles work in unison to produce fluid motion.

Animation for action games requires even more dedication. Animators routinely rely upon combat experts, often dressed in appropriate clothing, to stage mock battles. In this way, troop action can be recorded and studied, not only to show how the people move but also how their clothing and equipment reacts to that movement. According to Microsoft's Dangel:

> *[A typical day for an animator] is spent working with a character and bringing it to life. The specifics change from day to day. In the beginning of an assignment, the animator learns about how an entity will need to move through the world. They figure out what makes a character tick. Sometimes they bring other animators into the brainstorming process. Sometimes the art director, animation director, or lead game designer has specific requirements for the character, and those are ideally brought to light early on.*
>
> *From there, the animator creates a skeleton on which the character will move. Much like a puppeteer needs a variety of strings and levers to control a puppet, animators need [character rigging, which identifies where and how the character moves] to help them influence the motion of the character. It is common to spend a good amount of time setting up rigs just for this purpose. The rest of the time is spent addressing the motion needs of the character: making him or her run, walk, jump, slide, hop, kick, fight, etc.*

The day-to-day job of the entire art team is not to perfectly mirror reality but to create believable worlds from the past, or fantastic worlds of the future. Most important, these worlds should immerse the players into an environment that is believable and suspends his or her imagination while playing the game.

CAREER GROWTH

The art team is one of the most important and influential departments in the development of a computer game. Within the art department, there are a variety of jobs for people with varied skills, though even most entry-level positions require some experience with complicated design and animation programs.

If you choose to work on the visual side of computer game creation, you should learn to use as many of those previously mentioned software programs as you can. Background or texture map artists are common entry-level positions that earn around $25,000 to $30,000 a year. Even if you have skills to be a 3-D modeler or animator, it doesn't hurt to know about backgrounds, especially as many companies with small art departments will likely need artists to fill several roles. Modelers, 3-D artists, and animators will always make up the core of the art team, and these positions usually earn between $30,000 to $80,000, depending on overall experience and track record.

All of these positions can be stepping-stones to the position of art director, but smaller studios with tighter budgets don't always utilize dedicated art directors. In these cases, the game's lead designer, depending on his or her background, might instead fill the role of art director.

CHAPTER 8

SOUND DESIGNERS AND MUSIC COMPOSERS

While colorful, detailed, and realistic graphics are a huge part of the gaming experience, the game's sound effects heighten that experience further. The sounds of a gunshot, a sword clanking, or the howling wind of an empty field help immerse players into the game's environment, while background music also helps the game's graphics evoke the mood that the game's designers had in mind.

While computer graphics have certainly evolved, so have computerized sound effects. From the simple beeps and crashes of the 1980s, today's games have multichannel sounds, meaning that the sound can actually surround you. Musical scores in games have grown up from little more than rhythmic beats to lush melodies similar to movie soundtracks.

A sound designer works to assemble all of the auditory elements of the game by mixing the levels of the characters' voices and sometimes even composing the music. Most studios have libraries of recorded sound effects on CD, but there may be a need to go out with a DAT (digital audio tape) machine and record original sounds. A sound designer will also record all the dialogue in the game with voice actors. Some of this talent can come from Hollywood actors, for example, the use of the voices of Ray Liotta and Dennis Hopper in Rockstar Games' *Grand Theft Auto: Vice City*. Other times it can come from people already working in the studio. The makers of *Castle Wolfenstein 3D*, for example, lent their voices for the screams and shouts the bad guys make when you shoot them.

Recording sound is just part of the battle. You'll spend a good deal of time editing and sweetening the sound elements until they are the best they can be. Every sound designer works differently. Some will still use the traditional reel-to-reel tapes that were standard place in recording studios for decades, while others will take a more modern approach and record the sounds directly to a computer.

QUALIFICATIONS

Jack Grillo, audio director at Spark, is responsible for the sounds you hear in numerous games. He has provided sounds of dinosaurs in the PlayStation version of *The Lost World* and has worked on the noises and auditory chaos of virtual battlefields. Sound has always been a big part of his life.

"I started playing guitar and recording songs on an old four-track tape recorder when I was a teenager," explains Grillo. "A few years after college—I studied anthropology and music, at University of California at Santa Barbara—I decided to see how I could turn my interest in recording into something more. I began my sound design career as an intern at FranklinMedia, a small Los Angeles-based sound design company, back in 1996."

Many sound designers actually begin their careers as interns, and, like Grillo, this is where you'll learn as much about the elements of sound design as possible. This includes working with prerecorded sound effects available on CD-ROM, as well as those he had to create from scratch. Additionally, you'll learn about foley recording (matching sounds with existing visuals, such as hitting a piece of raw steak to mimic the sound of a punch), dialogue editing (synching up actors' dialogue with the characters on screen), and mixing (adjusting the sound of all the audio tracks). "I also had a chance to see how all of that worked in a few different mediums such as film, television, commercials, computer games," adds Grillo. "I eventually decided to concentrate on computer games and got a job with Electronic Arts Los Angeles in 2000. In 2002, I joined Spark Unlimited as the audio director, where I'm currently working on the *Call of Duty* series for Activision."

Sound designers should be grounded in both musicianship and sound effects. Some sound effects will be prerecorded, but many times the sounds that a game's designers want will have to be original. This could mean going to a shooting range to record gunshots, but more often than not, it requires simulating original sound effects. The need for the sound of a character that is walking on ice and snow doesn't mean a sound designer needs to take a plane ride to Alaska. He or she can re-create the sound anywhere by carefully bending a box of cornstarch and then using various audio effect processors in the studio to carefully change the original recording to mimic the desired sound effect.

For composers, playing an instrument and reading music aren't merely important; they're crucial. Understanding music composition—how different instruments complement each other to create harmonies and melodies —is also important. Knowledge of how computer and audio hardware interface (connect to each other and work together) is essential. Some software used in the industry includes Cakewalk, Sound Forge, Awave Studio, Pro Tools, and Vegas. Sometimes music composition means that a full band or even an orchestra will play each part, and other times it means you'll have to lay down—play and record—each of the individual parts via a computer or synthesizer.

"I went to college thinking I would become a recording artist and make a living as a jazz saxophone player," says David Henry, composer at Microsoft. After finishing college with a degree in jazz arrangement, Henry managed to get a job in corporate sales—not exactly his first choice but one that led to bigger and better things.

"[I wanted] to find a way to get a foot in the door, but it actually turned out to be [an] extremely valuable opportunity to get an understanding of how the business side of things worked, and I've been able use that experience to my advantage throughout my career." After about a year, a development team moved into an office where Henry was working and he soon learned that they were looking for someone to take care of audio. "It was a good opportunity for me, since they needed someone who had a background in arranging—but they needed someone to create arrangements of the music that would work with the game. That was really my big break into the industry."

As Henry and others confirmed, sound designers and composers must be willing to work as a team and take directions from the game's producers and designers. The ability to meet deadlines is also vital.

A Day in the Life of a Sound Designer

The career of a sound designer is anything but average. One day he or she might be recording the sounds of swords swinging through the air and the next he or she could be trying to find a way of simulating the creaks of an old wooden ship. Just coming up with the starting ground requires a lot of brainstorming.

Listening is where Jerry Martin, audio director for Maxis, gets his ideas. In fact, listening is usually the first step in creating the sounds you hear in games such as those from *The Sims* and *SimCity* series.

"Inspiration for sounds can come from anywhere. Sound designers are always listening to their environment. [They] are always on the lookout—ear-out—for sounds that can be used in new or unexpected ways. Most good sound design is not the sound of whatever object that it goes with. It's usually something that's totally different or in a lot of cases different sounds are mixed in with the real sound."

Good sound design not only adds realism to the game but also operates on a subconscious level. Hearing a rifle fire in a game shouldn't necessarily sound impressive, but it wouldn't work if it didn't sound appropriate to the visual cue. Making a sound that is as convincing as possible requires both skill and a good ear. A lot of this, says Spark audio director Jack Grillo, involves trial and error, but the real test comes in making everything sound good together.

"Creating the right sound is often the easiest part of my job. Getting them to play correctly [or at all] in the game is [a] different story altogether," says Grillo, who adds that much of his day is spent talking with dozens of team members including designers, animators, programmers, and producers. Sometimes he jokes that he spends half the day realizing he was talking to the wrong guy, but, he stresses, the process requires that he express himself clearly so that when he does find the right guy, they can work on a solution to any problem quickly.

In the end, using an existing or obvious sound effect versus one that is created requires different objectives. According to Grillo, both methods can be equally challenging.

I usually try to draw inspiration for my sound design choices from reality. If the game calls for a Thompson sub-machine gun, then my first move is to record the sound of that weapon. If the game calls for something that's a bit harder to come by, like a wizard's magic staff, I spend some time looking at the way the object behaves or I find out its intended use.

If the magic staff controls the weather, for example, then thunder and wind sounds will be the first sounds I experiment with. The next bit of inspiration comes from the sounds themselves. Every time I sit down to edit, I try to help each sound realize its own potential. Each sound has a unique quality, and each recording picks up different characteristics [based on weather conditions, microphone proximity, etc.] so the very process of listening to a sound can be all the inspiration I need. When I finally edit all the different sounds together, I take my inspiration from music, or at least I try to think like a music composer. Each sound should occupy a different spot in the frequency spectrum, so that when they occur, they complement one another, rather than cancel each other out. In battle sequences for example, I often imagine that the various weapons in a level are different sized drums, and their random combinations act as a sort of rhythm.

A DAY IN THE LIFE OF A MUSIC COMPOSER

For musical composers, the process can be even more involved. It used to be that a simple short loop of music was all that was needed to complement the action on screen. As games evolved, so did the accompanying music. Today the score—the background music—is as rich as that of a major feature film. Unlike a film where the score follows the action, music in games often has to be written to fit the course the player takes.

It is up to a music composer to get the right balance for a game and to make sure that its music reacts to the player but still flows naturally. Successful candidates will have extensive training in reading and composing music, as well as the ability to play an instrument.

Microsoft composer David Henry went to college thinking he would become a recording artist. Today he spends his days writing music for computer games such as the Xbox title *Crimson Skies: High Road to Revenge.* "*Crimson Skies* has several great examples of [the importance of a game's musical score]," says Henry. "While in an airplane in the open sky, if the player goes into a high-speed dive it is very difficult to provide a visual cue that says to the player 'You are going really fast now.' You aren't near any walls or surfaces and there may not be any other planes in the immediate vicinity, so you can't really do much more than a couple of camera tricks to give a sense of speed."

As a musical composer at Microsoft, Henry admits that the most important part of his job is to provide something that is there but isn't readily noticed. This isn't always easy. As a game's composer, he has to be just as creative as he had been while on stage as a sax player.

"It's very important for anyone doing audio to realize that if his [or her] work is good then it won't be noticed most of the time." The best game audio usually operates on a subconscious level—where it gives the players cues about the environment that they expect the real world to give them, but they have trained themselves to block out. "For instance," Henry continues, "people don't notice the [ambient] noise [in a room] or traffic noise, or general 'human' noises that they are constantly surrounded with, but when they are placed into an absolutely silent space they become extremely uncomfortable."

Most gamers don't even have an audio system capable of reproducing most of the work that he does. "The vast majority of gamers are still listening over PC or television speakers, yet for the past four to five years I've been doing just about everything in some surround [sound] format," Henry adds. "My philosophy on this is that while it's imperative to author so that everything is functional on a low-end system, I still optimize for the high-end user. I think they are more likely to care and appreciate the extra detail."

For some games, the music is less important, depending on the setting of the game. Many sports titles—especially those for the console systems such as the Xbox, PlayStation 2 and GameCube—actually try to mirror the experience that you'll see when watching these events on television. Performance-focused sports such as skateboarding often use background music, and thus the games try to emulate this interaction between music and sports.

Contemporary music is used for auto and other vehicular racing games because composed music might not be able to effectively keep pace with the action on the screen. These games instead rely on fast-paced music. The game's producer will seek out the appropriate tracks from new or established rock bands and rappers. Nile Rodgers, who has produced albums for Madonna and David Bowie, recently produced the soundtrack to Simon and Schuster Interactive's *Outlaw Volleyball* featuring new music acts such as Diffuser, Off by One, and Madcap. Rodgers believes that computer games are a great environment to break new talent that wouldn't ordinarily get a shot on radio, especially since gamers will be exposed to the same songs repeatedly as they play. Of course, it is just as likely that a hit song might find its way to a game, which can be very likely if the band happens to like games. As Nile Rodgers explains:

Artists need a viable voice. The perfect relationship for artists to have a place where their voices can speak without necessarily being censored or tapered or controlled is in the computer game world. A lot of the artists that I use probably would not have gotten on the radio. But when you listen to the records, you realize that any of these records could and probably should be on the radio. But radio is an environment now that the artistic community no longer controls. I can't walk into a radio station with a cool record and tell the DJ, "Check this out," and the DJ goes, "This is incredible; Thursday night, when I get my spot, I'm gonna stick it in." It [isn't] gonna happen. But I can walk into a computer game studio and go, "Guys, listen to this." And they'll go, "Wow, that's amazing." I can still do with computer game studios what I used to be able to do with radio stations.

When you come from a revolutionary culture like rock and roll, it seems [strange] to me that someone can dictate to you what's cool and what's not cool. Which is why being involved in computer games is exciting. It's revolutionary. Nobody's saying, "Absolutely not." That's how rock 'n' roll used to feel.

CAREER GROWTH

When it comes to creating the sounds and music for computer games, the typical formula usually involves doing everything at least twice. For sound designers, this might mean recording simple versions just to get the point across, while the composers will create a simple tune and see if it fits what the rest of the team had in mind. The producers and designers need to get a sense of what the results will be, and this usually means that the sound team will have to create "placeholder" sounds. These are bits of music and sound effects that are there just to give a rough idea of what the final piece might sound like, and as a result, the sound designers and composers are continually working to improve what has already been created.

This can be a rewarding process, but it can also mean tight deadlines. It is common for in-house sound designers to work in small teams and hire additional people as necessary. Thus, many people get in by working in a freelance capacity, eventually landing full-time jobs. On the flip side, some of the more successful sound designers are so good that they work for hire and go from project to project rather than being tied down to one game developer. Likewise, composers are often hired for one-time projects, which can sometimes lead to royalties from sales. This is a percentage of the profits from future sales, which can be

Tips from the Professionals

David Henry, Composer, Microsoft

The world of game audio can be a lonely place, and to be successful one needs to be [motivated]. On a team with ten artists and six programmers, it's not at all uncommon to have only one audio specialist. I'm really the only one on the team intimately familiar with audio production task lists, timeframes, and costs. If I fall down on the job there really isn't anyone who can easily pick up the pieces. I really like being in such a position, though—while the risks are high, I can claim nearly complete ownership of the successes. I find this inspires me and motivates me to be my best.

I work closely with all the different disciplines on the team at various times during a project. For scheduling and financial tasks, I work with the program manager and project leads. For audio implementation and other technical issues, I work with the developers, and I need to be in close sync with the art team so our creative direction meshes on a project. However, when it comes to tasks relating to audio creation, mixing, and procurement, I'm on my own. If I need input or feedback on some things (whether a music mix or specific sound has the desired impact for instance), I need to maintain a circle of resources outside my immediate team. I make sure to communicate with other people in the game audio business [other audio leaders, sound designers, composers, and voice directors] to keep up on new techniques and innovations, and to get "golden-ear" commentary on my own work.

Jack Grillo, Audio Director, Spark

On the sound design side, I think the most important learning experience for me was the sheer volume and variety of work I did for FranklinMedia. It was pure trial under fire, and because we were small, I had to know just a little bit about everything. The work ethic and flexibility I gained there has led me to be able to solve most of my current sound design issues quickly. I won't say that I'm never stumped, but at this point, I'm rarely surprised.

On the computer game side, my biggest learning experience was working within the team setting on Clive Barker's Undying *for EA. That project taught me that in order to become a good computer game sound designer, I would have to first become a clear and patient communicator.*

delivered monthly or annually, depending on the original contract agreement.

The salary range for full-time sound designers runs from around $45,000 to $68,000, depending on experience and education, as well as past successes. Sound designers who worked on a hit game will obviously be paid much more. Of course, when you're just starting out, you'll need to get experience. Many team members for sound design are hired as freelancers, meaning they aren't on staff, but instead are hired to work on a single project. Sometimes this means a few days' work, other times it might mean work for a few months. These types of positions are usually paid by the hour, and the rate can range from as little as $5.15 to $25 or more per hour.

Likewise, music composers can either work in-house or freelance, though usually only larger studios have in-house composers. In a staff position, a composer can make from $50,000 to $70,000, while freelance composers often begin as studio musicians for a project. A musician or music composer usually earns between $20 and $50 or more an hour, depending on his or her experience. A composer who can actually conduct a group of musicians will certainly make more money than a music composer who works alone with a computer.

Either way, the sound design and musical composition teams are integral to a game's development but are never in the spotlight as much as those working on the graphic design or programming. Because games are primarily a visual medium, sound designers and composers will often begin as a part of a small team and eventually move up until they are heading a larger group, or, at some development studios, a full department. However, without these people, games would not be nearly as engrossing as they are.

CHAPTER 9

THE PUBLICITY MACHINE

You don't have to work at a game company to be an industry insider. If you have good writing skills and can stick to tight deadlines, there might be a place for you in the press corps. For both public relations writers and journalists, the ability to work with a team, take direction, follow instructions, and meet deadlines is vital.

"When I first started working in this industry," said Nintendo's director of corporate communications, Beth Llewelyn, "people at magazines were [only writing] 'computer games are for kids.' Now look at any magazine; they have a games section."

Those game sections need writers, but it's not enough being able to write well. You'll have to write quickly, too. This is especially true if you work for a Web site or a publication that prints a weekly or daily publication. In addition to reviewing games, there is industry news to report, such as coverage of events, trade shows, and bits about upcoming gaming systems or the hottest titles.

Some writers begin as staff writers or assistant editors, while others write on a freelance basis. Either way, if you write clean copy (with few errors) and meet your deadlines, you will have a chance to move up the publishing hierarchy to a senior editorial position.

Once you master the skills of working in an editorial department (or have been writing steadily on a freelance basis), you will have the opportunity to move into public relations, or PR. PR is itself a whole mini-industry that works behind the scenes to make sure that the games get noticed in the stores and that the writers and reviewers hear about those "upcoming systems" and "hot titles." Free games are a great perk, but these jobs require more than fitting a controller in your hands—even if you are a reviewer!

QUALIFICATIONS

The qualifications for entry-level public relations specialists and journalists are similar. A university degree in journalism or communication will certainly help prepare you for a day-to-day job writing for a magazine or promoting a company. Public relations offices, such as any publishing company, are essentially media outlets, complete with editors and deadlines.

Most important, you must have solid writing and communication skills. Prepare to spend a lot of time on the phone, typing e-mails, and even sending instant messages. Organization is key. Be knowledgeable with basic computer programs such as Microsoft Word, Outlook, and Excel. Familiarity with a database program is especially helpful for individuals working in public relations. This is essentially where you store all of your press contacts.

To someone working in PR, these contacts are crucial. If you start as a writer, you need to build a list of industry professionals so you know from whom to get the information you need, whether it is obtaining a review copy, or just getting digital art to support your stories.

Game reviewers, even those who work in a freelance capacity, should play (or at least be acquainted with) computer games of all genres. It is important to remain objective, meet deadlines, and keep up-to-date on the latest trends. Not everyone has the same taste in games, but a reviewer needs to put personal feelings aside and examine both the qualities and faults of any game. A good reviewer can write about a racing game on one day, a role-playing game the next, and still be passionate about both. Many reviewers eventually move to select genres.

Public relations professionals act as the voice of a company and must work with magazines to set up necessary interviews, promotional events, provide review copies to the press, and even speak about company policy when necessary. While entry-level PR specialists mostly spend their time on the phone or sending e-mails, other members of the PR team might have to speak on television or answer questions at a press conference.

Taking college classes in communication, including public speaking, as well as having some media training is a plus. This is very useful when a PR specialist is needed to address awkward or difficult questions, such as why a game received a poor response from the public or has been delayed.

No matter which side of the phone you might be on, it is also important that you really know the computer game industry. This includes understanding the past as well as being able to anticipate the future. Dan Amrich, senior editor at *GamePro* magazine, says:

It's very important [to know the history of the industry], because it does tend to repeat itself. Knowing the past helps you identify trends. There are so many good books out on the history of computer games that there's really no reason to come into the fray without a fair grasp of that knowledge. Why was Atari so successful—

technology, culture, some of both? What helped Sony gain such a large market share, and what caused Sega to lose its own? There are reasons for these major events, and they're worth knowing.

Understanding where the industry is going means reading the trade magazines, which are publications specially written for and about the industry, as well as following business news and trends in technology.

A Day in the Life of a Magazine Editor

As you've learned in earlier chapters, a job in the computer game industry involves more than playing games. This holds true for computer game reviewers and editors, too. A significant portion of each day involves writing copy, be it an article, review, or interview, and then delivering it to another editor who revises it. The article then passes through a team of editors who make final corrections, at which time the magazine designers lay out the copy on the page. Since editors work many months ahead of the newsstand date, they usually work on several articles at once, each one in a different state of completion.

An editor can easily fill a good portion of his or her day holding meetings about what types of articles should appear in future issues and what images and screen shots (a picture of a computer game in action) are needed to illustrate the copy. Contact with game publishers, developers, and PR executives is an important way to learn crucial information about upcoming events and future games. "Yes, playing games is part of the job, too," says Amrich. "Most days I get to play an assigned game for a few hours, and it'll take a good week before I have enough playtime to build a valid critique."

Andrew Reiner, executive editor at *Game Informer* magazine, has been covering the industry for the past decade. He emphasizes that his life is much more than going into the office to play games.

That's what most people think I do. Sure, some days that's all I do, but the realization is that I have to write a story. It involves being creative, conveying every aspect of the game, and covering it in a way that the audience understands what I'm saying.

I have a lot of other stuff to do. I have to get screen shots, and other artwork. I'll talk to PR people and I'm generally busy. It isn't a nine-to-five job. It is an investment of time.

But, according to Amrich, surrounding yourself with games all day, every day, has its downside.

Some writers take on games as their job but then cannot handle it—their attitudes toward games change, they see them in a different light, and now what used to be their dream is a daily grind. Some folks burn out—and worse, some folks burn out and refuse to leave the industry, so they gripe bitterly and overreact in their reviews.

A DAY IN THE LIFE OF A PUBLIC RELATIONS PROFESSIONAL

Do you like to talk on the phone? That's a plus in the world of public relations. If you work in PR, either in-house at a computer game publisher or for a specialized PR firm, you'll be especially busy trying to get interest from journalists. You'll want to "book" them for an appointment at the trade show—but don't worry, you'll only be competing against every other company that attends the show.

The rest of the year you'll probably spend a lot of time on the phone as well. This involves making calls to see if the reviewers received the games you sent them. Then you'll need to call again to see if they'll be reviewing them. This process continues throughout the year. The busiest times are the weeks leading up to the annual trade show known as E3 (Electronic Entertainment Expo) and the weeks prior to and during the holiday season in November and December (when the majority of games are released).

But working as part of an in-house PR team at a computer game publisher versus an independent PR firm can be very different, according to Matt Schlosberg, public relations manager at Acclaim Entertainment:

As someone who's in-house, I am surrounded by games. Our team is involved in every step of the development process. It envelops you. In an external PR firm, a computer game company is just one client of many. You are detached from each client, whereas someone in-house might own stock in the company. We do a lot of in-house trafficking in terms of getting screenshots from the producers, but we also help out on a lot [of other things, too]. We're also brought in on company initiatives, whether it [involves] giving our input on new product ideas or finding out what market demographics apply to certain projects.

Making relationships is key. "The most valuable parts of E3 and CES [Consumer Electronics Show] to a computer games publicist are information gathering and community building," says Erica Kohnke, president and founder of Kohnke Communications, a San Francisco public relations firm that focuses on computer game clients. In addition to making sure that her clients' messages are told at these shows, she stresses that it is important to see what the other companies are doing and how their titles are being shown. Of course, she likes to know what the reviewers like. "It's important to build relationships with journalists with whom we have only met on the phone and over e-mail."

r e v i e w s

So that's what he looks like! A new third-person camera lets us finally see Garrett on the prowl. [below] Picking locks is more realistic, but still easy.

Silent and Deadly

*ION Storm quiets its critics with **Thief: Deadly Shadows**,*
a sequel every bit as good as its predecessors

★ ★ ★ ★ ⅟

BY BRETT TODD

IT'S NOT CRAP. ION Storm has brought down the curtain on years of fanboy negativity (It'll be dumbed down! It's being designed for consoles! Warren Spector sucks!) swirling around *Thief: Deadly Shadows* by producing a worthy heir to its classic predecessors. While grumps will no doubt gripe about mid-level loads breaking up the action and complain that missions aren't as big as they used to be, everyone else will be enjoying one of the best stealth games ever made.

Diehard taffers who loved the first two *Thief* games will find that little has changed thematically. The team at ION Storm has maintained the same melancholy mood, stealth-first gameplay, and signature graphical and audio touches that gave the two earlier games such personality. It's almost like original developer Looking Glass (R.I.P. 2000) has come back to life.

ION Storm has certainly picked up where its predecessor left off with the plot. Gruff but lovable cutpurse Garrett, once

52 COMPUTER GAMES | 08.2004

Magazines are an immediate source of information for gamers, such as this review of the stealth adventure series *Thief: Deadly Shadows*, a 2004 release by Eidos Interactive and Ion Storm. Magazines help to drive new games' publicity around the time of their release and are a common resource for gaming enthusiasts who are on the lookout for new challenges.

Kohnke also stresses that it's crucial to be as honest as possible, "I would abuse the trust of journalists if I were to repeatedly hammer them with low-grade games, insisting on their nonexistent superiority. I advise my staff to identify what is good about a game—what can honestly be said about this game to promote it?"

The day for PR professionals can be long, often starting before 9 AM and continuing late into the day. Because the majority of companies are located on the West Coast and many writers work on the East Coast, it's necessary to come into work early and stay late enough to take care of requests from West Coast team members and writers. In between phone calls, you will have to mail out copies of new games and press releases, maintain the contact list of journalists in a database, and liaison with production teams to get screen shots and other information. Sometimes the details fed to you by the producer are enough to compose a press release, a one- or two-page description of the product that highlights its important features. The producer might send an early version of the game to try out or a video of game footage to help.

The PR team will work on a strategy to maintain a game's "buzz." "There's a formulaic approach," explains Acclaim's public relations manager, Matt Schlosberg. You work with magazine editors to publish the first news piece about a game. In a few weeks, you will provide them with information for a quick preview. A hands-on preview follows—this includes playing through a few early levels in the game. Once the game is finished, the PR team will send a copy of it out for reviews and will extend coverage by giving out cheat codes. "Those are the basics," Schlosberg says. "You have to be creative: try an e-mail campaign where you break down a different feature of the game each week during the last couple of months leading up to the game's release." For a recent game, Schlosberg gave one magazine exclusive details to "break" a game. That means that he gave the magazine exclusive information. The result

Tips from the Professionals

Dan Amrich, Senior Editor, *GamePro* magazine
Realize that it's an insanely competitive industry and it won't be easy to turn someone's head. It's a cool job—therefore, everybody wants it. And since tons of people enjoy games, tons of people think they have the qualifications [to write about them]. Be prepared to follow up with everything professionally and thoroughly. It's a job, and you have a responsibility to be a voice of authority. Your opinions are your own, but because they are broadcast in some form, they hold weight, for better or worse. Be ready to accept that responsibility before you're lured in by dreams of having a massive collection of free games.

Know the style of the publication and nail it. Are you interested in getting a job writing about computer games, or are you interested in writing for GamePro? *If* GamePro *is your goal, learn what* GamePro *does differently (for better or worse!) and tailor your copy to match it. If you look like a good fit and you look like you understand that publication's specific approach, voice, and priorities, you stand a much better chance of making it there.*

Learn to edit your writing. If an editor asks for 250 words and you give them 280 because you "just couldn't cut anything," you won't be hired again because you have created more work for the editor. Being able to divorce yourself from what you've written and see the thirty words that have to go will make you much more employable.

Matt Schlosberg, Public Relations Manager, Acclaim Entertainment
[People interested in making a name for themselves in the PR world should] major in journalism with a concentration in public relations. Read press releases and try to write one of your own. Go to company Web sites. Look at the press releases there and find out who the PR contact is. It's usually listed at the top or very bottom of the release. Send a well-written cover letter and résumé to the contacts you've found. Go to E3, CES, stop by company booths, and hand out résumés. Not only does that show you want a job, but also that writing about computer games is your main interest. Going to a trade show demonstrates your willingness to find out the latest and most current news about the business. It shows that you're driven.

was a six-page story with interviews. "That started a lot of buzz," Schlosberg adds. Another tactic is to hold a PR stunt. These are elaborate, often bizarre events designed to generate a lot of press coverage quickly. To coincide with the release of *Turok: Evolution*, for example, the London office of Acclaim offered cash, an Xbox, and *Turok* games for anyone willing to change his name to Turok for one year.

CAREER GROWTH

Writing about games can be a very rewarding job, except in terms of money. A lot of people think it sounds great to play games, write about them, and travel around the country or world to see them being made. And because of these perks, many people are willing to do it for little or no compensation.

That doesn't mean you have to starve to make it as a game reviewer, but it does mean you'll have to work hard to get your name out there. Since most magazines won't hire writers without experience, the only way to get those first writing jobs is to work with little or no compensation. The best way to get that first writing job is to work without being paid. If you meet your deadlines, you'll probably get another assignment.

From that point, most writers establish relationships with several publications, eventually meeting various PR professionals who can keep your career rolling. You'll need to constantly network with other writers, PR folks from various game companies, software developers, and so forth. Every conversation could lead to a potential job. Watch out for negative speech. Keep an open mind. Meet other writers and share your leads—potential writing opportunities—with these professionals. While it might sound like you're giving away potential assignments, you're likely to hear about future writing possibilities in the process.

If you can devote the time to an internship at a magazine or PR firm, it's a great opportunity to make contacts and learn the ins and outs of the business. You'll learn about how a publishing company operates, potentially leading to future writing assignments. Most magazines and newspapers love to give the interns a chance to get real-world experience. Be sure to remain as professional as possible, and don't be disappointed if your internship doesn't turn into a full-time job.

Now the bad news: game reviewers in starting full-time staff positions don't get paid very well. An editorial assistant earns around $12,000 to $19,000. That's not a lot of money, but things can only get better from there. Magazines have numerous positions and each step up pays a little bit better. Full-time senior or managing editors make about $45,000 a year or more.

If you decide that working at a magazine isn't your thing, but you still like writing and working with the press, then a career in public relations might be a solid fit. Most PR firms have offices around the country, so even if a game publisher isn't in your town you're still likely to find an office near you. Most firms and internal PR departments are always in need of hardworking interns.

Once you land that first job, either at an independent PR firm or in the PR department of a game publisher, the work will be long and hard. The starting salary for PR coordinators or junior account executives is usually around $20,000 to $25,000. If you work hard and are enthusiastic, you're likely to be promoted quickly.

Account executives at a PR firm, who usually lead an account—meaning that they make most of the calls to the media while a coordinator mails packages—often earn more than $30,000 a year. From there you can be promoted to account manager, where you oversee an account and often keep in contact with the game's creators. Finally, you can move up to the director level, overseeing a couple of account managers. Salaries for these positions range from $50,000 to $70,000.

CHAPTER 10

THE FUTURE OF GAMING

With worldwide revenue at $20 billion, the electronic entertainment industry is truly global. It competes equally for people's leisure time with the music, television, and film industries.

Dedicated cable television networks, including Tech TV and G4 Media, have been launched to cover the world of consumer technology with a major focus on gaming. Most major computer-centric publishers, including Ziff Davis, IDG, FGN, and Bedford Communications, have magazines devoted to the game industry. Many major computer game publishers, including Activision and Electronic Arts, are publicly traded companies, watched closely by investment analysts.

Today we are also seeing the convergence of computer games with other forms of entertainment, especially Hollywood. It's getting harder to see where movies end and computer games begin. Gone are the days when the flesh-colored pixels of a game's hero would stand in for the Hollywood actor it was imitating. These days, realism rules. And games are not just taking their cues from pop culture, either; they're shaping it. After all, it's almost impossible to separate Tony Hawk the man from *Tony Hawk* the computer game franchise. The Matrix trilogy filmmakers, Andy and Larry Wachowski, worked very closely with Shiny Entertainment founder David Perry to make *Enter the Matrix* an integral part of the movie series, going so far as to write the script and shoot footage for the game while making the movie. Even the music business is now taking cues from the computer game industry.

No 'I' in Team

Once the product of rogue geniuses in their university computer labs, computer games are no longer created by single individuals but by teams of specialized employees. Communication between them is crucial, as is working—and playing—well with others. You must be dedicated to your vision but willing to adapt to an ever-changing market. As designer Alex Garden described, "At Relic we decided not to be the best game designer in the world, but rather to be real-time strategy designer." Relic made a choice to focus on one type of game and to do it well, whereas Electronic Arts is big enough to make a larger variety of titles.

You must know the market and the history of the industry. Computer games were being created and enjoyed before you were born, and they continue to evolve. Know the games and pay attention to trends. In the 1990s, games evolved from 2-D to 3-D. Today, AI is undergoing a radical shift toward greater sophistication. But despite the massive leaps in technology during the last thirty years, games generally rely on simple yet proven plots: boy meets girl, boy loses girl, boy shoots up bad guys to get girl back.

While creating games requires specialized skills, this doesn't mean you have to decide immediately what you want to do. Nor should you necessarily limit the skills you learn. A good graphic artist or animator might still know some of the fundamentals of sound design. The more you know, the further you'll go. In many small companies, everyone is expected to pitch in wherever needed.

"Game development these days is like making a movie," explains industry veteran Andy Eddy, author and editor. In his twenty years in the industry, he has seen it grow to the point that, today, there are myriad specialists working on a title. He recommends discovering what positions you are interested in and then focusing on, but not limiting yourself to, those areas. "Then, as corny as it sounds, after you've determined what you want to do, go to school. Few people can learn subjects such as 3-D programming and 3-D art techniques on their own to the advanced level that is needed to meet the requirements of a game publisher."

Even with the proper education, you shouldn't immediately expect a glamorous life turning your every whim into a computer game. It's a good idea to try to land a low-level game job, Eddy suggests, "such as a tester or intern, to learn what goes into making a game." Immersing yourself in a professional game-creating environment can be invaluable in learning about game development. Don't forget, Eddy adds, "to do some 'networking' for inside contacts that may be helpful in the future."

Even if the creative or technical process doesn't interest you, there are plenty of other possibilities for a career in games. "There are many ways to get into the games business beyond being a programmer," says Doug Lowenstein, president of the Entertainment Software Association (ESA). "There are opportunities for musicians, people interested in marketing, public relations, the law, and other fields."

VIOLENCE AND PIRACY

Every industry has its critics and hot-button issues. Computer games are no different. Today there are two primary concerns for publishers and developers alike. The first is the issue of computer game violence and the second is the games' ratings system.

Currently, every major publisher provides its games to the ESA, which in turn views the content and determines the appropriate age group (see the back of this book for full descriptions of the ratings). However, the ratings system still remains a confusing issue to the public, and this confusion has led to protests from various organizations as well as full-blown congressional hearings about computer games in Washington, D.C.

Not all games are violent shooters, but it is important to note that those types of games often tend to get more coverage than less violent titles. "Violence in games is certainly a hot topic," says Lowenstein, adding that he thinks that it is important for the industry to continue to innovate and provide a richer experience without unnecessary violence. "I hope that future game designers bring to the discipline an understanding that one can meet this challenge by creating better characters, better stories, and new genres rather than relying on tried and true formulas and violent images."

Likewise, better enforcement of the ratings system is crucial to the game industry's survival and future. "I do think that ratings will eventually be more effective," says Andy Eddy. "When you consider that the movie ratings have been in place since the mid-1960s, here we are about forty years later and everyone is aware of what the ratings do. The game ratings have been around for about a decade, and there's still a lot of refinement going on with the size, placement, information offered, etc. I think there's still an education about ratings that's in progress— not only with consumers, but with retailers—about how ratings will work in the process."

The other major issue for the game industry is piracy. As you can see after reading this book, a lot of people are needed to create a game, and every time a game is copied and shared, it means one less sale. If this trend continues, game budgets will decrease and the innovation in games will be greatly reduced.

"Piracy remains the single greatest challenge to the industry's growth," emphasizes Lowenstein, who stresses that the ESA operates a variety of programs to enforce the rights of game developers. But it is up to the gamer to help. "In the end, though, piracy will only be reduced to tolerable levels when all consumers show a respect for intellectual property."

David Cole, who predicts the worldwide computer game market will hit $30 billion by 2008, is president and founder of the industry analyst firm DFC Intelligence. He likens the piracy issue to squeezing Jell-O. "You fight on all fronts, but there's only so much you can do. It's always going to take a certain percentage. It's always going to be there."

For its GameCube, Nintendo used a smaller disc format than the standard five-inch CD or DVD, and that has helped it curb piracy, says Dan Amrich, senior editor at *GamePro* magazine. "Whether it's physical or digital, there is no perfect form of security—a determined pirate will take what he wants if only to say, 'I'm smarter than you.' So it's a question of how many obstacles you can put in the pirate's way, and then how many of those obstacles are also obstacles for legitimate users." Amrich cautions that if stringent piracy controls make gaming a hassle to consumers, another leisure activity will simply become more appealing.

Is the Future in the Palm of Your Hand?

The systems that your parents possibly played in their youth are dated by today's standards. The game machines that you likely enjoy today will be considered just as dated in the future. It is hard to imagine, but as technology moves forward, the cutting-edge systems of today are already in the process of being replaced.

Looking to the future, one thing is clear—computer games aren't going anywhere, though they might get smaller. Mobile phones and PDAs, including Pocket PC and Palm Pilot–based handhelds, could very easily be the handheld platforms of the future.

Handheld gaming is not new, having begun in the 1970s with simple electronic games that relied on monochrome LCD screens. But it was Nintendo's Game Boy system that arrived in the late 1980s that caused a phenomenon that hasn't stopped. As kids who grew up with a Game Boy or even the latest Game Boy Advance enter adulthood, they are still gamers. Armed with a cell phone or PDA, they will have a platform for playing rich games that might have just been an electronic dream twenty-five years ago.

Computer games have come a long way from the arcade halls. Today they are everywhere. "People who started out playing computer games are just now hitting thirty-five, and they're finding they're continuing to play even into adulthood," says analyst David Cole. With so many media besides PS2 and Xbox to get you playing: PCs, cell phones, PDAs, and Internet destinations such as Yahoo! Games, there's something for everybody. "Cell phone games are terrible," explained Dave Perry of Shiny Entertainment, "but they're better than boredom." Although the industry is relatively young (about thirty years old), it's starting to get respect. "My parents used to say to me, 'Are you finished with your games yet?'" Perry said. "I'm not playing games; I'm making games. This is a job."

GLOSSARY

AI Abbreviation for "artificial intelligence." Often refers to the ability of a computer to play a game against a human player. The computer controls all of the characters that a human player does not control.

bug A problem or error within a game's programming. It can be very minor, such as a wall that disappears when a character approaches, or very severe, such as crashing the game. A company's QA testers spend many hours searching for bugs, which programmers must fix before the game is finished.

buggy Relating to several problems that make a game difficult and unpleasant to play.

code The lines written for computer software in a programming language such as Visual C + + .

concept sketch A drawing, either on paper or the computer, of the way a character or environment will look based on the description in the design document.

console Consoles connect to the television set and play games exclusive to the system. PlayStation 2, Xbox, and GameCube are all game consoles.

crash A serious problem in the operation of a program that causes it to fail.

demo Typically, a free level or mission of a PC game that can be downloaded on the Internet so that players can try it out before they buy the complete game.

design document A paper or electronic document created and maintained by the design team. It contains information about a computer game's structure, such as its various levels of difficulty, what a player should accomplish at each level, and an overall summary of how the game will function.

environment The setting or "world" of a computer game.

first-person game Any game in which your point of view is identical to the character's.

flowchart A type of outline of a game detailing how the hero moves throughout the game's plot, including all his or her possible choices.

genre A style or category of games. For example, those that involve a 3-D world where the character is typically seen in third-person is an adventure game, or part of the adventure genre.

levels Different sections of computer games, which usually increase in difficulty as the game progresses. The linear structure of levels often requires beating a "boss" character to win the game.

level editor Sometimes called a layout editor, a level editor allows a designer to quickly place existing elements already created by the art department into the game. It is a tool that helps designers create the structure of the worlds the hero must navigate in any game.

mobile games These simple games run on PDAs, cell phones, and other portable devices.

mod An abbreviation for "modification." A mod is an alteration of a game, usually by a team of fans. For example, *Counter-Strike* is a multiplayer mod of the single-player game *Half Life*.

patch Some games shipped to stores still have bugs. These can be fixed with a patch, which is a separate program that fixes the problems in the original program (usually by overwriting certain original game files).

screen shots Still pictures of the game.

script A document written by the design team or a single designer or writer containing all the dialogue the characters will speak.

FOR MORE INFORMATION

Twenty Games Everyone Should Know

Pong (1975) Essentially computer tennis, games don't get much simpler than this: two paddles and a ball. The objective? Don't miss the ball. The game's inventor went on to found Atari.

Pac-Man (1980) Arguably the first real "character" in computer games, the Pac-Man character ate up dots on the screen while being chased by a variety of ghosts.

Donkey Kong (1980) Before we were introduced to 3-D Mario's extended family and pets, there was just 2-D Mario saving a 2-D girlfriend from a huge 2-D ape.

Zork (1982) Not the first text adventure, but the first great text adventure. You would read a descriptive paragraph of text and type in what you wished to do, "go east," for example. The text transported players to another world, and the game played out like a live *Choose Your Own Adventure* book.

Dr. J and Larry Bird Go One on One (1983) What started as a mere one-on-one basketball simulation actually launched computer game licensing (when a computer game company pays to use the likeness of a well-known character or celebrity in a game).

Dragon's Lair (1985) Using the cartoon artwork of Don Bluth, this coin-operated arcade game was the first to utilize Laserdisc technology. There wasn't really much in the way of fast-paced game play, but that didn't stop people from lining up to experience the rich hand-drawn animation.

Tetris (1986) In Tetris there are four different pieces that cascade down from the top of the screen. You must assemble them to create solid rows at the bottom.

Sometimes the simplest ideas are the best ones, and that certainly holds true with this classic.

John Madden Football (1988) There were football simulations before this one, but Madden changed the playing field forever. This long-running franchise has been available on many platforms.

Sid Meier's Pirates (1989) Long before *Grand Theft Auto III*'s open-ended adventures, this game let you do your thing your way. You could travel from port to port, fight off pirates, raid enemy cities and, if you are lucky, marry the governor's daughter!

SimCity (1989) It should be boring, right? Lay down water pipes, power lines, and commercial zones for a successful city? Somehow it works. All the little details, such as traffic congestion and earthquakes, add up to an addictive, rewarding experience.

Wolfenstein 3D (1990) It is hard to believe, but at one time action games were usually 2-D side-scrolling games. With this game, players could move around in a true 3-D setting—even if the graphics did occasionally cause motion sickness.

Sid Meier's Civilization (1991) Ambitious barely describes what this game attempted and actually succeeded to do. You start at the dawn of time in this turn-based simulation and lead your people to the near future, along the way exploring the world, expanding your civilization, and even exploiting other nations.

Doom (1993) *Doom*'s dark, moody atmosphere, combined with lightning-fast 3-D game play, blew away every other game on the market at the time. Big guns and scary monsters made for a winning recipe that is still followed today.

Dune II (1993) Today this is almost a forgotten classic, but it also launched the real-time strategy genre. Set in the fictional universe of the *Dune* novels, players battle each other while attempting to gather a single resource, which in turn is used to provide income to build structures and produce units.

Myst (1993) This was arguably the first "coffee table" game, a title that nongamers bought and played because of the lushly hand-drawn environments and detailed settings.

Tomb Raider (1996) Few computer game characters have transcended the medium enough to generate a full-length feature film such as the tomb-raiding Lara Croft. What could have so easily been a mere *Indiana Jones* clone spawned a cross-platform franchise.

Super Mario 64 (1996) Mario and his pals had been saving the princess for years, but this game added a 3-D element and helped make the Nintendo 64 console system a hot seller for the 1996 holiday season.

EverQuest (1999) This might not have been the first massive multiplayer online role-playing game, but it certainly is the most popular. It allowed you to create an alternate virtual life and be the hero you couldn't be in the real world, complete with quests to complete. Best of all, you could play with friends from around the world.

Grand Theft Auto III (2001) While its violent aspect might have drawn the most attention, this game's expansive worlds and open-ended game play, which had players take on the role of gangsters working for or against mob bosses, are what make it one of the most innovative games to date.

Battlefield 1942 (2002) This wasn't the first first-person shooter to let you control vehicles, but it was the first to make it completely balanced and utterly fun to play. You can drive tanks and fly planes, and when the World War II setting gets old, there are plenty of mods to keep this intense game play going on and on.

Some Key Players in the Industry

Dani Bunten, Berry
Notable games: *M.U.L.E.*, *Global Conquest*

Not all Hall of Fame–caliber computer game mavens are men. Dani Bunten's Berry games were considered ahead of her time, and, for the most part, she worked in an era without high-speed computers or high-powered consoles. *M.U.L.E.* was one of the first true multiplayer games ever created.

Nolan Bushnell
Notable games: *Pong*

The granddaddy of console gaming, Nolan Bushnell knew he was onto something when his first *Pong* machine overflowed with quarters from eager players. He went on to create the Atari home computer game system, which sparked the industry we know today.

John Carmack, id Software
Notable games: *Doom*, *Quake*, *Castle Wolfenstein 3D*

Widely considered the genius of the industry, Carmack first made a splash replicating Miyamoto's *Super Mario Brothers* on the PC. He programmed the first side-scroller for the PC, *Commander Keen*, and went on to revolutionize the PC industry again with the first 3-D game, *Castle Wolfenstein 3D*.

Richard Garriott, NCSoft
Notable games: *Ultima* series

After publishing his first game as a teenager, Garriott pioneered role-playing games with his *Ultima* series. Not just hack and slash adventures, players had to make moral choices that affected elements in the game.

Sid Meier, Firaxis Games

Notable games: *Civilization* series, *Railroad Tycoon*

Meier revolutionized the strategy genre. The best description of any of his games: addictive.

Miyamoto Shigeru, Nintendo

Notable games: *Donkey Kong*, *Mario* series, *Legend of Zelda* series

Hired as an artist, Miyamoto first made his mark on the game industry by designing *Donkey Kong*, a simple game in which a squat little man had to rescue his girlfriend from a giant ape. He later created the first side-scrolling game, *Super Mario Brothers*, in which the screen continued to scroll across as the player ran toward the edge of the monitor. For Miyamoto, fun takes precedence in a game's design, and many players have spent countless hours finding all the little hidden secrets in many of his games.

Will Wright, Maxis

Notable games: *SimCity* series, *The Sims* series

Best known for creating games of tasks that sound boring, Will Wright redefined how we approach games. *SimCity* simulated the running of a city—managing budgets, traffic flow, police response, and property values. It sounds dull, but Wright created a truly engaging experience, prompting us to forget about "beating the game."

Suzuki Yu, Sega

Notable games: *Hang On*, *Space Harrier*, *Virtua Fighter* series

What Miyamoto is to Nintendo, Suzuki is to Sega. Remember that old arcade game, *Hang On*, where players could actually ride a replica motorcycle while playing the game? That's his. He constantly strove for a balance between adrenaline and storytelling. *Space Harrier* was an old attempt at the creation of three-dimensional worlds. Most recently, he created the gigantic martial arts epic, *Shenmue*.

TRADE SHOWS AND CONFERENCES

These industry trade events are generally not open to the public, but it is possible for beginners and those wishing to get into the industry to attend.

American International Toy Fair

Web site: http://www.toy-tia.org

For more than 100 years, the American International Toy Fair has been the largest toy trade show in North America, attracting more than 1,500 manufacturers, distributors, importers, and sales agents from more than thirty countries.

Classic Gaming Expo

Web site: http://www.cgexpo.com

This show catalogs the history of computer games. It's a great place to meet industry legends and to brush up on yesteryear's favorites.

COMDEX

Web site: http://www.comdex.com

The focus of COMDEX is more on IT than games, but if you're in the area, it's a good place to check out the latest technology.

Consumer Electronics Show (CES)

Web site: http://www.cesweb.org

Since 1967, the Consumer Electronic Show, which is presented by the Consumer Electronics Association, has seen the introduction of some of the biggest home entertainment devices including the VCR, camcorder, and even Microsoft's Xbox.

D.I.C.E.

Web site: http://www.interactive.org/dice

Hosted by the Academy of Interactive Arts & Sciences, D.I.C.E. features two days of seminars by some of the industry's most creative minds, while also hosting the annual Interactive Achievement Awards ceremony.

Digital Hollywood
Web site: http://www.digitalhollywood.com

Events throughout the year address the convergence of computer games and Hollywood.

Electronic Entertainment Expo (E3)
Web site: http://www.e3expo.com/e3expo

This event celebrated its tenth anniversary in 2004. It remains the premier event for game developers and publishers to show off their upcoming titles to members of the press and retail buyers. Every year, E3 consists of several days of press conferences, workshops, and panels devoted to entertainment and educational software.

Game Developers Conference (GDC)
Web site: http://www.gdconf.com

This conference remains the official trade event put on by game developers for game developers. GDC features more than 300 lectures, panels, tutorials, and roundtable discussions on game development with leading industry experts. The conference also features the annual Independent Games Festival, where new unpublished games compete for the attention of publishers.

MacWorld
Web site: http://www.macworld.com

Everything with even a passing relationship to Apple Macs, including games, is at this show.

SIGGRAPH
Web site: http://www.siggraph.org

An annual conference for computer graphics, including computer games, animation, and art.

Tokyo Game Show (TGS)

Web site: http://tgs.cesa.or.jp/english

Every year, this international trade show features the latest technology and business trends in electronic entertainment, including mobile phone and online games as well as developments in console systems.

ESA INFORMATION AND MEMBER COMPANIES

Acclaim Entertainment, Inc.
One Acclaim Plaza
Glen Cove, NY 11542
(516) 656-5000
e-mail: esa@theesa.com
Web site: http://www.acclaim.
  com

Activision
3100 Ocean Park Boulevard
Santa Monica, CA 90405
(310) 255-2000
Web site: http://www.activision.
  com

Buena Vista Games
500 South Buena Vista Street
Burbank, CA 91521-8174
(818) 553-3923
Web site: http://www.
  buenavistagames.com

Capcom USA, Inc.
475 Oakmead Parkway
Sunnyvale, CA 94085
(408) 774-0500
Web site: http://www.capcom.com

Crave Entertainment
19645 Rancho Way
Rancho Dominguez, CA 90220

(310) 687-5400
Web site: http://www.
  cravegames.com

Eidos Interactive
651 Brannan Street
San Francisco, CA 94107
(415) 547-1200
Web site: http://www.eidos.com

Electronic Arts
209 Redwood Shores Parkway
Redwood City, CA 94065-1175
(650) 628-1500
Web site: http://www.ea.com

Entertainment Software Association (ESA)
1211 Connecticut Avenue, NW #600
Washington, DC 20036
Web site: http://www.theesa.com

id Software
3819 Towne Crossing, Suite 222
Mesquite, TX 75150
(972) 613-3589
Web site: http://www.
  idsoftware.com

Konami Digital Entertainment —America
1400 Bridge Parkway
Redwood City, CA 94065
(650) 654-5600
Web site: http://www.konami.com

LucasArts Entertainment Company
1600 Los Gamos, Suite 200
San Rafael, CA 94903
(415) 472-3400
Web site: http://www.lucasarts.com

Microsoft Corporation
One Microsoft Way
Redmond, WA 98052
(425) 882-8080
Web site: http://www.xbox.com

Midway Games, Inc.
2704 West Roscoe Street
Chicago, IL 60618
(773) 961-2222
Web site: http://www.midway.com

Namco Hometek, Inc.
2055 Junction Avenue
San Jose, CA 95131
(408) 922-0712
Web site: http://www.namco.com

Nintendo of America, Inc.
4820 150th Avenue NE
Redmond, WA 98052
(800) 633-3236
Web site: http://www.nintendo.com

NovaLogic, Inc.
26010 Mureau Road, Suite 200
Calabasas, CA 91302
(818) 880-1997
Web site: http://www.novalogic.com

SEGA of America, Inc.
650 Townsend, Suite 600
San Francisco, CA 94103
(415) 701-5000
Web site: http://www.sega.com

Sony Computer Entertainment America (SCEA)
919 East Hillsdale Boulevard
Foster City, CA 94404
(650) 655-8000
Web site: http://www.playstation.com

Square Enix USA, Inc.
6060 Center Drive, Suite 100
Los Angeles, CA 90045
(310) 846-0400
Web site: http://www.squaresoft.com

Take-Two Interactive Software, Inc.
575 Broadway, 3rd Floor
New York, NY 10012
(212) 334-6633
Web site: http://www.take2games.com

THQ, Inc.
27001 Agoura Road
Calabasa Hills, CA 91301
(818) 871-5000
Web site: http://www.thq.com

Ubi Soft Entertainment
625 Third Street, 3rd Floor
San Francisco, CA 94107
(415) 547-4000
Web site: http://www.ubisoft.com

Vivendi Universal Games
100 Universal City Plaza
Universal City, CA 91608
(818) 777-1000
Web site: http://www.vivendiuniversal.com

WildTangent
18578 NE 67th Court, Building 5
Redmond, WA 98052
(425) 497-4500
Web site: http://www.
  wildtangent.com

Check out the Computer Game
Yellow Pages (http://www.
vgyellowpages.com) for a
comprehensive directory of
the industry.

University and College Programs

Contact these schools for
information on their degree
programs, course catalogs, and
admissions information. If
possible, visit a college or two
and ask for a tour.

American Film Institute
2021 North Western Avenue
Los Angeles, CA 90027
(323) 856-7600
Web site: http://www.afionline.
  org

Art Center College of Design
1700 Lida Street
Pasadena, CA 91103
(626) 396-2200
Web site: http://www.artcenter.edu

Art Institute of Phoenix
2233 West Dunlap Avenue
Phoenix, AZ 85021
(800) 474-2479
Web site: http://www.aipx.com

The Art Institutes
Free Markets Center
210 Sixth Avenue, 32nd Floor
Pittsburgh, PA 15222
(888) 624-0300
Web site: http:// www.
  artinstitutes.edu

Brooks College
4825 East Pacific Coast Highway
Long Beach, CA 90804
(562) 597-6611
Web site: http://www.
  brookscollege.edu

California Institute
1200 East California Boulevard
Pasadena, CA 91125
(626) 395-6811
Web site: http://www.caltech.edu

California Institute of the Arts
24700 McBean Parkway
Valencia, CA 91355
(661) 255-1050
Web site: http://www.calarts.edu

Carnegie Mellon University
5000 Forbes Avenue
Pittsburgh, PA 15213
(412) 268-2000
Web site: http://www.cmu.edu

Cerro Coso College
3000 College Heights Boulevard
Ridgecrest, CA 93555
(760) 384-6100
Web site:
http://www.cerrocoso.edu

Cogswell Polytechnical College
1175 Bordeaux Drive
Sunnyvale, CA 94089
(800) COGSWLL (264-7955)
Web site: http://www.cogswell.edu

College of Media Arts and Design at Drexel University
3141 Chestnut Street
Philadelphia, PA 19104
(215) 895-2386
Web site: http://www.drexel.edu

Collins College
1140 S. Priest Drive
Tempe, AZ 85281
(480) 966-3000
Web site: http://www.houseofedu.com

DePaul University
1 East Jackson
Chicago, IL 60604
(312) 362-8000
Web site: http://www.depaul.edu

DeVry University, West Hills
22801 Roscoe Boulevard
West Hills, CA 91304
(818) 713-8111
Web site: http://www.devry.edu

DigiPen Institute of Technology
5001-150th Avenue NE
Redmond, WA 98052
(425) 558-0299
Web site: http://www.digipen.edu

Full Sail Real World Education
3300 University Boulevard
Winter Park, FL 32792
(800) 226-7625
Web site: http://www.fullsail.com

Georgia Institute of Technology
Atlanta, GA 30332
(404) 894-2000
Web site: http://www.gatech.edu

Illinois Institute of Art
1000 North Plaza Drive
Schaumburg, IL 60173
(847) 619-3450
Web site: http://www.ilis.artinstitutes.edu

Indiana University
107 S. Indiana Avenue
Bloomington, IN 47405
(812) 855-0661
Web site: http://www.indiana.edu

Madison Area Technical College
3550 Anderson Street
Madison, WI 53704
(800) 322-6282
Web site: http://matcmadison.edu/matc

Massachusetts Institute of Technology
77 Massachusetts Avenue
Cambridge, MA 02139
(617) 253-1000
Web site: http://web.mit.edu

Mercy College
555 Broadway
Dobbs Ferry, NY 10522
(800) MERCY-NY (637-2969)
Web site: http://www.mercynet.edu

Michigan State University
409 Communication Arts Building
East Lansing, MI 48824
(517) 355-8372
Web site: http://www.msu.edu

Minneapolis College of Art and Design
2501 Stevens Avenue South
Minneapolis, MN 55404

(612) 874-3700
Web site: http://www.mcad.edu

Montana State University
PO Box 172180
Bozeman, MT 59717-2180
(888) MSU-CATS (678-2287)
Web site: http://www.montana.edu

New York Institute of Technology
1855 Broadway
New York, NY 10023
(800) 345-6948
Web site: http://www.nyit.edu

New York University
70 Washington Square
New York, NY 10012
(212) 998-1212
Web site: http://www.nyu.edu

Northwestern University
633 Clark Street
Evanston, IL 60208
(847) 491-3741
Web site: http://www.
  northwestern.edu

Parsons School of Design
66 Fifth Avenue
New York, NY 10011
(212) 229-8959
Web site: http://www.parsons.edu

Philadelphia University
School House Lane
Philadelphia, PA 19144
(215) 951-2800
Web site: http://www.philau.edu

Platt College
6250 El Cajon Boulevard
San Diego, CA 92115
(619) 265-0107
Web site: http://www.platt.edu

Pratt Institute
200 Willoughby Avenue
Brooklyn, NY 11205
(718) 636-3600
Web site: http://www.pratt.edu

Rhode Island School of Design
Two College Street
Providence, RI 02903
(401) 454-6100
Web site: http://www.risd.edu

**Ringling School of Art
  and Design**
2700 North Tamiami Trail
Sarasota, FL 34234
(800) 255-7695
Web site: http://www.rsad.edu

**Rochester Institute
  of Technology**
One Lomb Memorial Drive
Rochester, NY 14623
(585) 475-2411
Web site: http://www.rit.edu

San Francisco State University
1600 Holloway Avenue
San Francisco, CA 94132
(415) 338-1111
Web site: http://www.sfsu.edu

San Jacinto College Central
8060 Spencer Highway
PO Box 2007
Pasadena, TX 77505
(281) 476-1501
Web site: http://www.sjcd.cc.tx.us

**Savannah College of Art
  and Design**
342 Bull Street
Savannah, GA 31401
(800) 869-7223
Web site: http://www.scad.edu

School of Communication Arts
3220 Spring Forest Road
Raleigh, NC 27616
(919) 981-0972
Web site: http://www.sca3d.com

School of Visual Arts
209 East 23rd Street
New York, NY 10010
(212) 592-2000
Web site: http://www.
   schoolofvisualarts.edu

**Seattle Central
   Community College**
1701 Broadway
Seattle, WA 98122
(206) 587-3800
Web site: http://www.
   seattlecentral.org

Southern Methodist University
PO Box 750181
Dallas, TX 75275
(214) 768-2058
Web site: http://www.smu.edu

**University of
   Advancing Technology**
2625 West Baseline Road
Tempe, AZ 85283
(602) 383-8228
Web site: http://www.uat.edu

University of Baltimore
1420 North Charles Street
Baltimore, MD 21201
(401) 837-4200
Web site: http://www.ubalt.edu

**University of
   California, Berkeley**
Department of
   Computer Science
Berkeley, CA 94720
(510) 642-6000
Web site: http://www.berkeley.edu

University of California, Irvine
Irvine, CA 92697
(949) 824-5011
Web site: http://www.uci.edu

**University of California,
   Los Angeles**
405 Hilgard Avenue
Box 951361
Los Angeles, CA 90095-1361
(310) 825-4321
Web site: http://www.ucla.edu

University of Colorado, Boulder
Boulder, CO 80309
(303) 492-1411
Web site: http://www.colorado.edu

University of Colorado, Denver
Campus Box 167
PO Box 173364
Denver, CO 80217
(303) 556-5600
Web site: http://www.cudenver.edu

University of Indiana
107 South Indiana Avenue
Bloomington, IN 47405
(812) 855-4848
Web site: http://www.iub.edu

**University of
   Massachusetts, Lowell**
One University Avenue
Lowell, MA 01854
(978) 934-4000
Web site: http://www.uml.edu

University of Michigan
Ann Arbor, MI 48109
(734) 764-1817
Web site: http://www.umich.edu

University of Missouri
Columbia, MO 65211
(573) 882-2121
Web site: http://www.missouri.edu

University of North Texas
PO Box 311277
Denton, TX 76203
(940) 565-2000
Web site: http://www.unt.edu

University of Southern California
University Park Campus
Los Angeles, CA 90089
(213) 740-2311
Web site: http://www.usc.edu

University of Texas at Austin
1 University Station
Austin, TX 78712
(512) 475-7348
Web site: http://www.utexas.edu

**University of Texas
  at Dallas**
PO Box 830688
Richardson, TX 75083
(972) 883-2111
Web site: http://www.utdallas.
  edu

University of Washington
1410 NE Campus Parkway
PO Box 355852
Seattle, WA 98195
(206) 543-9686
Web site: http://www.
  washington.edu

**Virginia Commonwealth
  University**
Richmond, VA 23284
(804) 828-0100
Web site: http://www.vcu.edu

ORGANIZATIONS, JOB SITES, TRADE MAGAZINES AND NEWSLETTERS

ORGANIZATIONS

Association for Computing Machinery (ACM)

Web site: http://www.acm.org

The industry's leading portal to computing literature and conferences. ACM runs SIGGRAPH, an annual conference on computer graphics.

1515 Broadway
New York, NY 10036
(800) 342-6626

Association of Shareware Professionals (ASP)

Web site: http://www.asp-shareware.org

Founded in 1987, the ASP has been dedicated to the advancement of shareware as an alternative to conventional retail software.

Entertainment Software Association (ESA)

Web site: http://www.theesa.com

1211 Connecticut Ave., NW #600

Washington, DC 20036

Entertainment Software Rating Board

Web site: http://www.esrb.org

The ESRB provides ratings to help parents and other consumers choose the games that are right for their families.

Interactive Entertainment Merchants Association (IEMA)

Web site:http://www.iema.org

Founded in 1997, the IEMA is the retailer trade group.

NPD Funworld

Web site: http://www.ndpfunworld.com

The NPD Funworld provides sales and marketing information for the computer industry.

Software & Information Industry Association (SIIA)

Web site: http://www.siia.net

The SIIA is the principal trade association for the software and digital content industry and provides global services for intellectual property protection.

JOB SITES

Gamasutra, http://www.gamasutra.com

Game Industry Biz, http://www.gamesindustry.biz

Game Industry News Job Site, http://www.gignews.com/
  jobs
GameJobs, http://www.gamejobs.com
Game Recruiter, http://www.gamerecruiter.com

TRADE MAGAZINES AND NEWSLETTERS

Game Developer Magazine
CMP Media LLC
600 Harrison Street, 3rd Floor
San Francisco, CA 94107
Web site: http://www.gdmag.com

Game Industry News
Web site: http://www.gameindustry.com

Game Market Watch
Web site: http://www.gamemarketwatch.com/

GameDAILY Newsletter
Gigex, Inc.
1 Sutter Street, Ste 500
San Francisco, CA 94104
Web site: http://www.gamedaily.com

WEB SITES

Animation Arena, http://www.animationarena.com
FlipCode, http://www.flipcode.com
Game Design, http://www.gamedesign.net
GameDev, http://www.gamedev.net
Game Development Central, http://www.gdcentral.com
Game Programmer, http://www.gameprogrammer.com
modding, http://www.thefreecountry.com
Programmer's Heaven, http://www.
  programmersheaven.com

Programming Tutorials, http://www.
programmingtutorials.com

THE RATINGS SYSTEM

As the Motion Picture Association of America assigns
ratings such as "PG" and "R" to movies, the Entertainment Software Ratings Board (ESRB) does the same to
computer games. The ratings are as follows (courtesy of
http://www.esrb.org).

EC (Early Childhood) Content that may be suitable
for people aged 3 and older. Titles in this category
contain no material that parents would find
inappropriate.

E (Everyone) Content that may be suitable for people
aged 6 and older. Titles in this category may contain
minimal violence, some comic mischief, and/or
mild language.

T (Teen) Content that may be suitable for people aged 13
and older. Titles in this category may contain violent content, mild or strong language, and/or suggestive themes.

M (Mature) Content that may be suitable for people
aged 17 and older. Titles in this category may contain
mature sexual themes, more intense violence, and/or
strong language.

AO (Adults Only) Content suitable only for adults. Titles
in this category may include graphic depictions of sex
and/or violence. Adults Only products are not
intended for people under the age of 18.

RP (Rating Pending) Title has been submitted to the
ESRB and is awaiting final rating.

ESRB CONTENT DESCRIPTORS

alcohol reference Reference to and/or images of
alcoholic beverages.

animated blood Cartoon or pixilated depictions of blood.

blood Depictions of blood.

blood and gore Depictions of blood or the mutilation of body parts.

cartoon violence Violent actions involving cartoonlike characters. May include violence where a character is unharmed after the action has been inflicted.

comic mischief Scenes depicting slapstick or gross vulgar humor.

crude humor Moderately vulgar antics, including "bathroom" humor.

drug reference Reference to and/or images of illegal drugs.

edutainment Content of product provides user with specific skill development or reinforcement learning within an entertainment setting. Skill development is an integral part of product.

fantasy violence Violent actions of a fantasy nature, involving human or nonhuman characters in situations easily distinguishable from real life.

gambling Betting-like behavior.

informational Overall content of product contains data, facts, resource information, reference materials, or instructional text.

intense violence Graphic and realistic-looking depictions of physical conflict. May involve extreme and/or realistic blood, gore, weapons, and depictions of human injury and death.

mature humor Vulgar and/or crude jokes and antics, including "bathroom" humor.

mature sexual themes Provocative material, possibly including partial nudity.

mild language Mild references to profanity, sexuality, violence, alcohol, or drug use.

mild lyrics Mild references to profanity, sexuality, violence, alcohol, or drug use in music.

mild violence Mild scenes depicting characters in unsafe and/or violent situations.

nudity Graphic or prolonged depictions of nudity.

partial nudity Brief and/or mild depictions of nudity.

sexual violence Depictions of rape or other sexual acts.

strong language Profanity and explicit references to sexuality, violence, alcohol, or drug use.

strong lyrics Profanity and explicit references to sex, violence, alcohol, or drug use in music.

strong sexual content Graphic depiction of sexual behavior, possibly including nudity.

suggestive themes Mild provocative references or materials.

tobacco reference Reference to and/or images of tobacco products.

use of alcohol The consumption of alcoholic beverages.

use of drugs The consumption or use of illegal drugs.

use of tobacco The consumption of tobacco products.

violence Scenes involving aggressive conflict.

FOR FURTHER READING

DeMaria, Rusel and Johnny Lee Wilson. *High Score! The Illustrated History of Electronic Games.* Berkley, CA: McGraw-Hill Osborne Media, 2002.

Gershenfeld, Alan, Mark Loparco, and Cecilia Barajas. *Game Plan: The Insider's Guide to Breaking In and Succeeding in the Computer and Video Game Business.* New York: St. Martin's Griffin, 2003.

Olesky, Walter. *Coolcareers.com: Video Game Designer.* New York: The Rosen Publishing Group, Inc., 2000.

O'Donnell, Annie. *Coolcareers.com: Computer Animator.* New York: The Rosen Publishing Group, Inc., 2000.

Weigant, C. *The World of Work: Choosing a Career in Computers.* New York: The Rosen Publishing Group, Inc., 2000.

BIBLIOGRAPHY

Asakura, Reeiji. *Revolutionaries at Sony: The Making of the Sony PlayStation and the Visionaries Who Conquered the World of Video Games*. New York: McGraw-Hill Professional Publishing, 2000.

Boardman, Ted. *3DS Max 6 Fundamentals*. Indianapolis: New Riders, 2003.

Burnham, Van and Ralph Baer. *Supercade*. Boston: MIT Press, 2001.

DeMaria, Rusel and Johnny Lee Wilson. *High Score! The Illustrated History of Electronic Games*. Berkley, CA: McGraw-Hill Osborne Media, 2002.

Gershenfeld, Alan, Mark Loparco, and Cecilia Barajas. *Game Plan: The Insider's Guide to Breaking In and Succeeding in the Computer and Video Game Business*. New York: St. Martin's Griffin, 2003.

Johnston, Ollie, and Frank Thomas. *The Illusion of Life: Disney Animation*. New York: Hyperion Press, 1995.

Kent, Steven L. *The Ultimate History of Video Games: From* Pong *to* Pokemon—*The Story Behind the Craze That Touched Our Lives and Changed the World*. New York: Prima Lifestyles, 2001.

King, Brad, and John Borland. *Dungeons and Dreamers: The Rise of Computer Game Culture from Geek to Chic*. New York: McGraw-Hill Osborne Media, 2003.

King, Lucien, ed. *Game On*. New York: Universe Publishing, 2002.

Kushner, David. *Masters of Doom: How Two Guys Created an Empire and Transformed Pop Culture*. New York: Random House, 2003.

LaMothe, André. *Windows Game Programming for Dummies*. New York: For Dummies, 2002.

Llopis, Noel. *C++ for Game Programmers.* Hingham, MA: Charles River Media, 2003.

Olsen, Jennifer. Gamasutra.com, 2003 Game Development Salary Survey. Retrieved February 11, 2004 (http://www.gamasutra.com/features/20040211/olsen_01.shtml).

Sellers, John. *Arcade Fever, The Fan's Guide to the Golden Age of Video Games.* Philadelphia: Running Press, 2001.

Sheff, David and Andy Eddy. *Game Over: Press Start to Continue.* San Francisco: GamePress, 1999.

Steed, Paul. *Modeling a Character in 3DS Max.* Plano, TX: Wordware Publishing, 2001.

Takahashi, Dean. *Opening the Xbox: Inside Microsoft's Plan to Unleash an Entertainment Revolution.* Roseville, CA: Prima Lifestyles, 2002.

Turcan, Peter and Mike Wasson. *Fundamentals of Audio and Video Programming for Games.* Redmond, WA: Microsoft Press, 2003.

William, J.F. *William's Almanac: Everything You Ever Wanted to Know About Video Games.* Toronto, ON: Isabelle Quentin, 2002.

INDEX

ABOUT THE AUTHORS

Dave Gerardi is a writer, editor, and filmmaker. His work has appeared in two dozen publications, including *FHM* and *Newsweek*. He has covered electronic entertainment, film, celebrity culture, and toys.

Peter Suciu is a New York–based freelance writer who has covered trends in consumer electronics, technology, electronic entertainment, and the toy industry for more than a decade. In that time, his work has appeared in more than three dozen publications including *Newsweek*, *PC Magazine, Wired,* and the *New York Daily News*. He is married to fellow freelance writer Enid Burns and lives in a crowded New York apartment with their two cats.